Duke Ellington

JAZZ MASTERS SERIES

Duke Ellington

PETER GAMMOND

First published in Great Britain in 1987 by
APOLLO PRESS LIMITED
11 Baptist Gardens, London NW5 4ET

British Library Cataloguing in Publication Data
Gammond, Peter
  Duke Ellington.—(Jazz masters series; 10)
  1. Ellington, Duke   2. Jazz musicians—
  United States—Biography
  I. Title   II. Series
  785.42'092'4   ML410.E44

ISBN 0-948820-00-4

Series editor: David Burnett James

Typesetting by Concept Communications
(Design & Print) Ltd. Crayford, Kent

Printed and Bound in Great Britain by
Anchor Brendon Limited, Tiptree, Essex

Contents

Illustrations

The publishers thank Roy Burchell and *Melody
Maker* for access to their files.

Foreword

When tackling a demanding subject like Bach or Schubert or Duke Ellington, one is generally inclined, either through trepidation or modesty, to apologize for shortcomings. I don't intend to apologize much, for I have said about Duke Ellington what I genuinely feel; and most of it is based upon deep and intuitive affection rather than the usual aggressive defence attitudes that are to be found in much jazz writing. If I had any doubts it was that my view of Ellington was an old-fashioned one that makes me admire his earlier periods, in spite of genuine effort, so much more than his later work. Because of this, I am deeply grateful to Burnett James, who went far beyond the bounds of his duties as series editor, in re-shaping some of the text; often, I am pleased to say, supporting my opinions, but occasionally modifying them or persuading me to a more balanced view. Although the book is fundamentally mine, he has acted more as co-writer than as mere editor. Beyond that it is impossible even to begin to thank all those friends and associates with whom I have enjoyed discussing Ellington; or all those who have written stimulating things about him. Beyond this, my main thanks must go to the Duke himself. My own brief acquaintance with him was a final delight to add to the years of pleasure I have had from his music. I can only hope that my assessment, however wayward, will at least steer a few more faltering steps towards the same rich enjoyment of his great and undying legacy.

PG.

The Piano Player

To those whose tastes developed during the fifty-year long golden age that we now refer to as the Ellington era, it seems incredible that Duke Ellington is no longer around; has, indeed, already been dead for more than a decade. The oldest jazz fan alive (who shall, tactfully, be left unnamed) may still just remember the emergence of the Ellington sound in the 1920s. But already the youngest will have been born too late to have heard that great musical chameleon, the Ellington orchestra, in the flesh. A decade or so is a comparatively short time in which to settle our thoughts on such a big and long lasting subject. In a hundred years' time it will be much easier to encapsulate the total Ellington achievement, to give him his proper rank as a composer, when judgement has been helped by the contractions of time. Today, while memories can just about be said to be fresh, we can only make a personal attempt at summing up the past and estimating the future position of Ellington in jazz and overall musical history. It is hardly long enough as yet to take an unemotional view.

Supposition is not a desirable ingredient of history; but it has its uses in argument. Let us suppose that Ellington had simply been a pianist; just another black musician emerging in the early days of jazz acceptance. Our task would have been to persuade the world of the talents of a very unusual player. Perhaps, by now, we can see more clearly that the prejudices of earlier days that left him constantly underrated in this role have been over-balanced by estimates which may lean too far the other way. In the perspective of his total achievement there is really no point in being over vehement with claims that he was of the highest rank. He did not leave many virtuoso solos behind so that we could assess him alongside the likes of Earl Hines, Art Tatum, Erroll Garner or Oscar Peterson. If opportunity and inspiration arose he could launch into a gutsy swinging solo in the old James P. Johnson style. Mainly, his solos had a thoughtful, probing quality about them. Ellington's playing was the aural sketchbook of a composer; sensitive, questing and imaginative; very rarely dull, repetitive or static. The fact that the interest in his work lay in its ideas rather than in technique or display would have perhaps always stood in the way of him becoming a popular soloist.

Within the band's performances and recordings we soon realize that Ellington's statement of themes, developments and variation, neatly inserted between instrumental sections, either as solos or linking passages, are very much the skeleton of the total concept. As he plays there is a sense of probing, gently pushing, experimenting. And often, though there was no doubt much premeditation behind it, there is a sense of improvization that always kept his music laced with the accepted spirit of a jazz performance. At the piano, he would often state the theme, suggest what was to be done with it, show the possibilities for later development—all within the space of eight or sixteen bars. The rest was a matter of dressing up these basic thoughts in the rich orchestral colours he had at his disposal. There was a fascinating record available, which is not often listed as an essential part of the Ellington collection, on which Duke plays in a duet with Earl Hines. The contrasting roles of orchestral catalyst and virtuoso executant are absorbingly demonstrated here on the track called *House of Lords*. Hines, naturally, is the dominant partner in terms of notes played and sheer skill: Ellington, as he would in his band, simply propels the whole thing along. Yet, without in the least underrating the contribution of one of the greatest of all jazz pianists, Earl 'Fatha' Hines, it may be said that it is often Duke Ellington who draws attention and whose contribution is, possibly, in the end, the most constructive and compelling.

As a jazz musician, general and extraordinary rather than specifically as a pianist, an assessment of Ellington's achievement is complicated by the fact, to put it bluntly (and, not beyond possibility, wrongly) that he may well have been forced (but also may have wanted) to pursue his career beyond its ideal span. Had his years of activity been those of his peak period (let us say from 1935 to 1950, with a little leeway either side) it is quite possible that his work would have hit us with even greater impact than it has done in its widely dissipated actuality. While some may justifiably disagree, it has seemed to many of his admirers, certainly the bulk of those who wrote about his later recordings and concerts, that Ellington's music was no longer the vital force it had been. Not because it was any less accomplished or that his later soloists were lesser men than his earlier ones or less creative or imaginative; but because the Ellington style was no longer flourishing in the natural social and cultural environment that had inspired it. His music was a product of the late 1920s and the 1930s and came to one of its great peaks in the early 1940s just as jazz was breaking away from its origins. The original impetus lasted well into the 1950s. Ellington never made the mistake of trying to change his basic style to something that was foreign to his nature; but his later work often seemed to lack the natural authority of the earlier music. It could even sound like a careless parody of itself, and Ellington was often guilty of writing out the original lyricism of some of his creations.

It may be putting things the wrong way round to say that Ellington came into jazz history just at the right time for what he had to offer. Like virtually all truly original creative artists, Duke Ellington was both a child and a creator of the times in which he lived. If the times helped to form him, he more than helped to form the times, certainly the artistic times, the current climate and environment, social as well as artistic. He was there, as were others, to offer the growing art of jazz firm guidance as it left the carefree New Orleans days behind. He offered intelligence, imagination and organization to an often undisciplined music. He showed, in a number of directions, what jazz was capable of. He showed in particular what the big band had to offer, not simply by being, in time, a part of the Swing Era (his art was always too subtle for that) but by demonstrating superbly that jazz was was not just 'hot' sounds and rhythmic excitement but a field for real creative activity where lasting compositional master-pieces could be produced by means of the unique musical resources jazz possessed.

The idea that Ellington outlived his peak is not only based upon an assessment of his personal position. Because he was part of the big

A Duke Ellington jam session: (l to r) Brad Gowans, Juan Tizol, Cootie Williams, Eddie Condon and Rex Stewart.

band era his most telling legacy was to big band jazz. But, sadly, by the end of his career even that was no longer a viable musical outlet. The type of jazz that Ellington and others was creating is now more or less extinct except for a few nostalgic re-creations. For a time a few continued—Kenton in America, Dankworth in England; Basie survived him for a while, and Buddy Rich still fronts a show case for his own drumming. But no one surpassed what Ellington had done at his best and Ellington himself never progressed beyond what he had achieved in his peak periods. In any case, the Ellington band differed from most others in that it was primarily a composer's rather than an arranger's band: it existed in the first place to play its leader's compositions; it was kept in being even through the most difficult years when for economic as much as if not more than artistic reasons, big bands virtually disappeared from the scene and even Basie had to resort to a small group for a while. Though the Ellington band played for dancing, for shows and concerts, since, like every other it had to earn its living out on the stands and please the paying customers, its true *raison d'être* was to present Ellington's own music. He always said that he was not interested in what happened to his music in the future; he wanted to hear it there and then, and that was why he kept the band going, even when it cost him money and caused endless worry. It was his way of subsidizing his own works.

It would be gratifying to be able to assume that, when those writers in a hundred years time are assessing Ellington and our primitive jazz world they will be looking back at Duke as an early master of jazz composition; a Vivaldi or a Haydn at least, if not a Mozart or a Beethoven. The Mozarts and Beethovens of jazz now seem unlikely to appear. Those who saw jazz as a new outlet for serious musical expression have been disappointed. Jazz has made its impact, a total impact on the world of popular music; but it has never properly or wholly impinged on the world of what musical snobs like to think of as 'serious' music. It was assumed by various tentative and often confused writers of the 1920s and 1930s that jazz, in its more profound aspects, as typified by such divergent figures as Duke Ellington and George Gershwin, might well forge a link between the worlds of 'serious' and 'popular' music. Briefly, in the early heydays of both these figures, it seemed a possible if not necessarily a probable (or, to some desirable) development.

In fact, quite the opposite happened, simply because of the awfulness of most of the hybrid efforts that materialized. The basic truth is perhaps that jazz can never be a wholly written-out music. Even within the settled framework of an orchestra like Ellington's, with a distinctive creative mind like his behind it, the essence of a jazz composition is still what happens in performance. In one sense this is true of all music: it is what the Spanish composer long resident in England, Roberto Gerhard, implied when he said that performance is 'the moment of truth'. The expressiveness of jazz cannot be set down on paper. Popular music, where the same improvisatory element now prevails, took over the jazz language, so that today virtually all popular music is to a greater or lesser extent jazz based. The potential links between 'classical' music and jazz finally disappeared when the jazz idiom that Ellington had written for, the big band, became itself a dodo while the classical world that might have been ready for the jazz flavour, i.e. the audience that used to welcome regular new symphonies and operas found that virtually nothing new was appearing that they could understand or enjoy. The so-called 'jazz influence' on certain contemporary composer in the 1920s, like Stravinsky, Martinu, or Walton, was in the truest sense superficial, concerned almost solely with surface effects and a few rhythmic derivations, and, like snakes in Ireland, virtually did not exist, despite a certain amount of specious propaganda. Concert audiences now spend most of their time listening to old music, much on the same principle that made William Hazlitt declare, 'Whenever a new book appears I read an old one.' A reactionary and obstructionist attitude, no doubt; but also an understandable one in the circumstances.

Even the kind of composer whose works, while difficult, might mellow into acceptability in a decade or so is a thing of the past, since figures like Stravinsky have gone. Today there is virtually no creation of truly popular 'classical' music; and perhaps there has not been since the passing of such once universally acclaimed figures as Elgar, Sibelius and Richard Strauss; or perhaps in certain specific examples, Mahler. Most of what is produced today, in whatever genre, and including jazz, will never reach more than a minimal intellectual audience. Both 'serious' music and jazz have become increasingly introverted and academic and of minority appeal.

Current popular music has always been aimed at a young audience, but the pop music of today is even more specifically orientated towards a teenage market which primarily loves noise, a heavy beat, and surface excitement. Because it often has no great musical or expressive depths, it now has to be supported with visual gimmickry, which may range from electronic juggling to erotic gymnastics. The performers wear grotesque costumes and makeup and do all they can to keep their audiences' minds off the music by constant physical gyrations. And a video background, in whatever context, is gradually becoming an essential adjunct. Beyond this, the only universal outlet for popular music of a more adult flavour is the musical theatre.

The flourishing theatrical connection with contemporary popular music makes it even sadder that Ellington never managed to put his full powers into a successful musical which, containing songs and instrumental numbers up to his most exalted standards, might well have turned out to be another *West Side Story* or *Porgy and Bess*. His one or two more or less tentative sorties into this arena, like *Jump for Joy*, and his collaboration in others, give a few tantalizing glimpses into what might have been.

The Duke steps out

Duke Ellington was born in Washinton DC on 29 April 1899. He was christened Edward Kennedy; the Edward after his father James Edward Ellington, Kennedy the maiden name of his adored and beautiful mother, Daisy. When his parents were first married they lived with his maternal grandmother who was the wife of a Captain of Police and had raised a family of ten children. By the standards of most jazz lives, it was an eminently respectable background, 'a wonderfully warm family life' as Duke himself later described it, where he was loved and pampered and generally 'spoilt rotten' by all the women in a well-to-do home. In this he resembled that other famous band leader of the early days, Fletcher Henderson, who also came from an economically stable middle class family.

Duke's father, in the early days, worked as butler in the house of a well known doctor and the contacts made there led to opportunities to cater for various social functions. A pleasant offshoot of this was that the Ellington family always had the very best of good food. Perhaps this was the origin of his formidable and famous appetite which lasted throughout his life. (There is a story about a time before the war when the band was in Paris, and a rather earnest party asked trombonist Joe 'Tricky Sam' Nanton, somewhat portentously, if 'Mr Ellington' was a genius; and Tricky put on that melancholy look of his and retorted: 'Genius? I don't know about that. But Jesus, can he eat!')

Later, during World War I, Ellington senior gave up his career as butler and concentrated on catering, at one time for the U.S. Navy, where he also worked on blueprints. He retired when he began to suffer from arthritis.

There always seemed to be an adequate supply of money around and Edward Kennedy was given good schooling and, revealing some musical talent, was given piano lessons by a lady teacher. But at first his interests lay more in sport and art. At school he acquired the nickname 'Duke', an acknowledgement of his confident manner and smart way of dressing. He modelled himself on his father who was a colourful talker, a great dancer, a wine buff, a wit and a flatterer of women (this latter was another legacy which lasted all through Duke's life and found expression many times in his music. He was a sucker for a pretty woman, a sophisticated lady, and his music reflects it). He was also brought up with a deep belief in God, especially by his mother. Both parents played the piano, respectable and often sentimental drawing room pieces and operatic selections, and their efforts inspired him, as a boy in 1914, to write a piece, a tribute to a spare time job he had in the Poodle Dog Cafe, called *Soda Fountain Rag*. His second composition—*What you gonna do when the bed breaks down?*—already seems to indicate a modest revolt against his respectable upbringing. As a teenager he frequented pool rooms and clubs with his school friends and was earning a modest reputation as a pianist. Washington in the immediate post-war years seemed to be full of pianists, some of them conservatory trained, and these Duke respected. But it was what he called the 'unschooled' that attracted him most, the ragtime pianists who vied with each other in 'cutting contests' in the local clubs. Ellington was a great listener and he absorbed all that he heard of such pianists as Louis Brown who, he remembered, had an 'unbelievable technique' and the expert Doc Perry who showed him a technical trick or two and how to ornament and improvize. There were others around too, such as Lester Dishman, Clarence Bowser, a great 'ear-man', Sticky Mack, Louis Thomas, Caroline Thornton, Roscoe Lee and Gertie Wells. Ellington remembered them all.

He became a 'relief' pianist, taking over minor jobs that one of the other pianists couldn't fit in. At a local dance hall he found it created a good impression if he made exaggerated movements of the hands, like Luckey Roberts whom he heard and saw at the Howard Theatre. There is a picture from those days of Duke Ellington playing in the Washington DC cabaret of Louis Thomas. The drummer is Sonny Greer.

Before he left high school he had won an art scholarship, and for a time his piano was in the background. But the musical jobs were soon flowing in on a regular basis. In those days Ellington described himself as a 'champion drinker' but he became rather abstemious in later life. To keep up his reputation he was forced to learn to read and write music properly. The Ellington bands then were both small and fluid.

The great James P. Johnson came to Washington to play at the Convention Hall. When he played his *Carolina Shout,* a piece Duke regularly performed, Ellington was egged on to challenge the great man. Johnson was very kind about his young rival's performance and a lasting friendship began. Ellington always felt indebted to James Percy Johnson for his early encouragement.

The nucleus of Duke's first Washington bands was a family of brothers, the Millers, who played guitar, drums and trombone. Later his schoolfriend Otto Hardwick joined them, first playing bass but later switching to C-melody saxophone. Another local aspirant was another school friend, trumpeter Arthur Whetsol, and on banjo there was Elmer Snowden. At this time too, Duke met Juan Tizol, a member of a touring band that visited Washington. These familiar names suggest that Ellington was adept at adopting styles to his purpose, rather than the other way round. Importantly, in 1919 drummer Sonny Greer reappeared in Washington fresh from a stint with a trio led by Fats Waller. Greer had been to New York and told them many stories of his experiences there and of the great names in jazz who flourished in the big city. So when Greer landed a job in New York with the Wilbur Sweatman band, the rest of the Washingtonians followed. Waiting for the work to come in, they would spend their evenings listening to Willie 'The Lion' Smith at his Capitol Palace club and to Fats Waller at the Orient. Ellington himself was frequently allowed to sit in with the great ones. The other boys made their living meanwhile playing pool. Duke did his own housework and repairs and kept himself as immaculate as his nickname demanded.

From 1923 to 1926 there were many ups and downs, followed by a fairly settled time at the Kentucky Club. Then, in 1927, they auditioned for an engagement at the famous Cotton Club on Lenox

Avenue in Harlem. Six other bands responded and turned up on time. Ellington and his group arrived late—and so did the manager of the club. Theirs was the only band he heard, and they got the job.

The Cotton Club has now been fed back into the world of general public awareness by a highly romanticized and expensive screen epic produced by Francis Coppola. It has been portrayed, as almost every other subject with a musical or jazz background has been, in exaggerated dramatic terms. Otherwise it would not be box office. The Cotton Club, in those far off days of prohibition and gangster rule, was very much an integral element in the formation of the Ellington style.

The first club to inhabit the premises on the corner of 142nd Street and Lenox Avenue in Harlem was the Douglas Casino. In 1920 it became the Club Deluxe under the management of the former heavy-weight champion Jack Johnson. It was taken over, behind the scenes, by the Owen Madden gang as an outlet for their bootleg beer and other more potent drinks. The Club was now refurbished in a style that was considered attractive to the rich and thirsty white customers that the syndicate wanted to pull in. The choice of the name Cotton Club is of uncertain origin, but it had enough of the privileged 'white only' tinge about it, together with a suggestion of black plantation style entertainment to give it an unpleasantly loaded reputation and atmosphere. It was given a jungle decor and until about 1927 the entertainment was mainly provided by black artists and musicians imported from Chicago. The food was Harlem style with Chinese and Mexican touches. The Club celebrated its grand opening in 1923 with a Negro stage revue, slick, commercial, fast-moving, glamorous, revealing. The material was written by songwriter Jimmy McHugh amongst others. High standards of behaviour were maintained to avoid too much police investigation. Unruly customers were ejected. They were strictly white (or, at most, but palely coloured) and it attracted a snobbish element. It was dubbed by Lady Mountbatten 'the aristocrat of Harlem clubs'. Even so, the police managed to catch the club on its prohibition law violations and it closed in 1925.

It re-opened in 1926 with new management and a new revue produced by a director called Dan Healy who set out to make the show even slicker and faster than before. In 1927 it was decided that Chicago based entertainment was not good enough. A name band must be brought in. The job was offered to King Oliver and his Dixie

Syncopators. He turned it down, strangely on the grounds that the money was not sufficient, for the Cotton Club was the highest paying place in Harlem. Jimmy McHugh suggested the Ellington band, but his suggestion was not received with enthusiasm. So the historic audition was called.

By 1926, the Washingtonians lineup was—Rudy Jackson, Percy Glascoe, Fred Guy, Toby Hardwick, Sonny Greer, Edgar Sampson, Joe Nanton and Bubber Miley. For the Cotton Club engagement Ellington enlarged to an eleven-piece band and the familiar lineups of the years from 1927 onwards began to settle into place. Duke himself has said that in those days it was expected that a band should be led and directed by a violinist, so they hired one—but the idea was not a success.

The Cotton Club, daringly exploiting 'black' entertainers, was one of those places, expensive and 'classy' that catered for the rich; one of the few clubs in Harlem where the 'white' audiences went. The performers were well paid. There was a regular chorus of twelve dancing girls and eight singers, 'all beautiful chicks'. The entertainment and music provided had to be demonstrably 'black' in the most primitive sense. It was here that the Ellington 'jungle' sound was created, the African element emphasized in a way that might seem somewhat distasteful today. The air was full of tom-toms and gongs, with Miley and Nanton growling away on their horns like lions in the undergrowth. The credit side of all this was the superb music that Ellington created and was able to create out of such necessity, richly rewarding when all the undertones of race are conveniently forgotten.

Some six months after Ellington's arrival in New York he had met an astute businessman-cum-publisher and would-be singer called Irving Mills, who gradually took over management of the band. Some jazz historians are inclined to be unkind to Mills on various counts, not least his singing. Ellington summed him up as a 'clever man' and has acknowledged that it was Mills who made him realize that it was his own music that it was most important to plug and record. It was the efforts of Mills that got them their later club, theatre and film engagements at a time when there was still much prejudice against black bands. Mills had to fight hard to get the Ellington records into the general catalogues of the recording companies, to have the band accompany famous white artists, to get into the film lots, to tour in comfort in the South, even to get Ellington into

ASCAP (American Society of Composers, Authors and Publishers). But by 1930 the Ellington band was successful and respectable (it was even 'famous' on record labels), and it was Mills who organized the first visit to England in 1933 with appearances at the London Palladium and, as Ellington always delighted in emphasizing, meetings with the Royal Family. He was not called Duke for nothing.

Residence at the Cotton Club meant that the band became widely known from the radio programmes that regularly went out from there. In 1929 they had also played for Ziegfeld's *Show Girl* with a score by George Gershwin. In 1930 they accompanied Maurice Chevalier at the Fulton Theatre, the band also featuring a selection of Ellington pieces. They appeared with Amos 'n' Andy in a filmed version of a popular radio feature *Check and Double Check* and made popular hits of the Ruby-Kalmar number *Three Little Words* and an Ellington-Mills composition called *Ring Dem Bells*. Two pleasant little Ellington legends of the time, concern firstly, *Mood Indigo*, which assumed its proportions of a chamber piece (originally called *Dreamy Blues*) because half the band were late for a recording session; and, secondly, *Creole Rhapsody* which became the first larger work in the Ellington output when Mills lightly referred, at a press conference, to what was then only intended as another three-minute item, as 'part of a larger work—a rhapsody'. Ellington thought he had better live up to the claim. He wrote such a lengthy piece that they had to record two versions—a shorter one for Brunswick and a longer one for Victor. Mills had a lot of arguing to do before he could persuade either company to record a jazz number that took up two whole sides and more. It set the pattern for future 'extended' works, though Ellington was never wholly to shake off the early discipline of the three-minute 78 rpm records. Most of his extended works were suites that were simply a string of such pieces with a co-ordinating theme. There were exceptions, like *A Tone Parallel to Harlem*; but that was the general rule. It is something that was not always recognized and has caused some misunderstanding of the real nature of his longer works.

The Irving Mills coup of an appearance at the London Palladium, organized with Jack Hylton, really set the band on its international path. They pulled out all the theatrical stops for this visit to the world's No. 1 variety theatre. Ivie Anderson thrilled the audiences with *Stormy Weather,* the Harold Arlen hit from the Cotton Club; Bessie Dudley danced seductively to *Rockin' in Rhythm,* and there was polite enthusiasm for *Mood Indigo*. Even in those days the British critics—foremost among them, as an Ellington appreciator, Spike Hughes—did not find the Ellington stage presentation as replete with pure jazz as it might (and, so they thought, should) have been, and demanded an evening of serious jazz-making. The *Melody Maker* organized a Sunday concert at the Trocadero cinema at the Elephant and Castle, with all the British dance band world taking up a large percentage of the seats. They were there to learn. Ellington remembered that it was taken so seriously that Spike Hughes took up space in his review to criticize the audience for clapping in the middle of numbers. Duke and the band were astonished to discover how well known they were in Britain.

In the press, the influential 'Needlepoint' of *Melody Maker*, during a sustained controversy on the merits of black music, had frequently remarked, in company with others, that black bands could not swing. For a time remarkably few Ellington records were reviewed in those august pages. But by 1933 the appreciation of true jazz was blossoming. Ellington was appreciative of the way that 'the most distinguished British composer of the period' (his judgement), Constant Lambert, had written understandingly about their recordings. Lord Beaverbrook threw a big party to which the Prince of Wales and the Duke of Kent came. The Duke of Kent showed his knowledge of Ellingtonia by asking for *Swampy River*. The Prince of Wales, who fancied himself as a drummer, watched Sonny Greer all night. Said Ellington: 'The atmosphere in Europe, the friendship, and the serious interest in our music shown by critics and musicians of all kinds put new spirit into us and we sailed home in the *Majestic* in a glow that was only partly due to cognac and champagne.'

On their return to the US they played in Chicago during the World Fair and toured Texas. In 1935 Daisy Ellington died, and Duke was inconsolable for a long time. In her memory he wrote *Reminiscing in Tempo*. At the Cotton Club in 1937 *Caravan*, written by and featuring Juan Tizol, was a new hit and created a vogue for this kind of exotic material. In 1938 James Edward Ellington died, and Duke's old friend Arthur Whetsol became too ill to continue with the band. Following the rewarding trip to England in 1933, the middle 1930s were not a happy time for Ellington on the personal plane, however well his career in music may have been going.

In 1939 Ellington and Mills decided to part and Ellington

The Duke Ellington band as featured in the 1942 film Cabin in the Sky. *Photo: Max Jones files.* (l to r, back row) Otto Hardwick, Juan Tizol, Harold Shorty Baker (with trumpet), Harry Carney, Johnny Hodges, Al Sears, Joe Nanton. (l to r, middle row) Ray Nance (below Baker), Ivie Anderson (vocalist), Rex Stewart, Ben Webster, Wallace Jones, Lawrence Brown, Sonny Greer. Front row: bass and guitar not seen; and Duke on piano.

illustrated the loss of this guiding hand by writing a revue *Jump for Joy* which was designed 'to fight Uncle Tomism in the entertainment world'. It lasted for only twelve weeks after playing to half empty houses. To revive their spirits after that they gave a concert at Carnegie hall. Next, a recording ban imposed by James C Petrillo to try to force all musical outlets to use union members now almost bankrupted the band which was losing a substantial amount weekly. They were saved when a cheque for $22,500 arrived on account of royalties on the song *Don't Get Around Much Any More*. Such was the value of having so many different irons in the fire.

By the 1940s a number of the original Ellington musicians had died or left the band for one reason or another. There was a period when Ellington seemed to have lost the art of writing distinctive songs and instrumental pieces. The jazz world was leaning towards bop and much of what was heard had already been looked into by Ellington. When he returned to England in 1948 he found a very different world from 1933. Food rationing was still in force. This time he did not bring the whole band with him—the Musicians Union ban on American and other foreign bands was operating and strictly enforced. He came, much to all jazz fans' disappointment, as a sort of vaudeville act, his own piano playing augmented by the rather frail art of singer Kay Davis, who had appeared on some of the band's recordings, and the trumpet/violin playing and other talents of Ray Nance. Ellington would play a medley of his popular songs, the favourite standby, and then Nance would indulge in mimicry on his instruments, sing like Sammy Davis and tap dance with astounding agility. Again there were some more jazz-orientated performances arranged with a group of English musicians to provide the backing. But somewhere in all this there was the grain of misguided taste that has been a weakness in the Ellington saga throughout. It has several times been demonstrated by his choice of unsuitable singers to go with the band. Only Ivie Anderson ever really satisfied the jazz buffs in this respect. There is no reason, of course, why Ellington or anyone else should only play what certain other people decide is 'jazz'. Significantly, Duke himself had said, while resident at the Cotton Club: 'We didn't think of it as jazz; we thought of it as Negro music.'

At the end of the '40s another recording ban kept the band out of the studios. Again he was losing some of the excellent musicians that he had trained up to replace the originals, such as Tyree Glenn who had become the stalwart of the trombone section. And it was near the end of the partnership with Sonny Greer, who was suffering from poor health. The 1950s started with a crisis for most American bands and long established groups such as those led by Count Basie and Woody Herman were forced to reduce or temporarily disband as the economic situation in America worsened. The Ellington band managed to survive and in 1950 started on a European tour. Don Byas joined the saxes for this to patch up any temporary weakness in that department; and the tour took them to Sweden, France, Denmark and Switzerland. Some sessions for the new Mercer label were followed by some more for Columbia, historic in two ways. They were the first to be recorded with the Long Playing record in mind and included lengthy versions of *Sophisticated Lady*, *Mood Indigo* etc, plus a new extended work, *The Tattooed Bride*. Secondly, they were to be the last records for some time with Johnny Hodges, Lawrence Brown and Sonny Greer, who were all departing to form a band under Hodges's leadership. Hodges and Brown eventually returned to the Ellington ranks, but Greer never did though he had many active years ahead of him and died at an advanced age. The new star of the band was trumpeter Harold 'Shorty' Baker.

In 1951 Ellington premiered his *Harlem Suite* (otherwise *A Tone Parallel to Harlem*) at the Metropolitan Opera House. An association with Capitol records in the mid-1950s led to some rather precious music-making and some up-dated reworkings of old standards such as are to be found on the 'Ellington '55' album. By the summer of 1955 the band was back with its vaudeville stunts playing in a Acquacade show on Long Island with two harpists and a string section. Thoughts that the Ellington band might be dying of lack of imagination were dispelled when Hodges returned and two excellent LPs were recorded for the Bethlehem label in 1956. Later in the same year Duke was back with Columbia and had a new, if rather astonishing, hit with a more or less impromptu jam session at the Newport Jazz Festival based on the old (1937) *Diminuendo and Crescendo in Blue*, in which tenor-saxophonist Paul Gonsalves played innumerable frenetic choruses that were as primitive a demonstration of jazz power as anything put on record. It vulgarized and effectively ruined one of Duke's finest conceptions; but it certainly put Ellington back on the map.

But even now there was a rift between the rather pretentious leanings of Ellington and his supporters' club. His 1957 potted jazz history, *A Drum Is a Woman,* was generally sneered at by the critics although it contained some lovely rich writing and sound worthy of the 1940s band. A suite based on Shakespearean characters, *Such Sweet Thunder,* took jazz, in the words of Oscar Hammerstein II, 'about as far as it could go', a noble effort to compose jazz of a highly literate standard which succeeded because the jazz spirit was all-informing.

The band's visits to Europe and England in 1958 were again marred by the now expected wrongful application of double standards. Treated to a fare that consisted of the eternal 'song medley' (if mercifully without indifferent vocalists) and pretentious mood music, the jazz fans clamoured for the old works of merit and some good jazz from what was now once more a potentially great band with the impressive lineup of—Ray Nance, Harold Baker, Cat Anderson, Clark Terry (t); Quentin Jackson, Britt Woodman, John Sanders (tb); Johnny Hodges, Harry Carney, Russell Procope, Jimmy Hamilton, Paul Gonsalves (reeds); Sam Woodyard (d); Jimmy Woode (b), plus the regular piano player. It was 25 years since the last visit of the full band, different though it now was, and the Ellington afficionados came with the highest expectations. One sensed a slight edge of disappointment among the more intelligent customers. There were great moments without doubt. *Mood Indigo* sounded as good as ever and several of the old masterpieces retained their magic. There was Johnny Hodges, still as majestic, and the old Harry Carney sound. Most impressive of the 'new boys' was Clark Terry who, though modern in tone, seemed to have inherited the 'vocalized' trumpet tradition. On the other hand, Cat Anderson's squeals, often like a nasty car skid, seemed to add nothing imaginative and one uneasily wondered why Duke used such sounds. This time too it seemed to take a concert or two before Ellington realized yet again that the British fans wanted the jazz and not 'magnolias just dripping with molasses' however much, in the words of Stanley Dance, these new works showed 'an adventurous imagination, ranging eagerly beyond the confines of popular song.' There were plenty of people beyond the confines already doing just that. Anyway, as the tour progressed the music got better and better.

One sensed that even more of the inspiration than one had perhaps recognized stemmed from the man at the piano. As Hugues Panassié put it in our Ellington symposium, it was at the piano that Duke 'talks the music that others will play'. If the Duke was in a gutsy mood and period that was how the band would be; if he was in a fanciful and hi-falootin' mood, so would the band be. Ruby Braff went further to say: 'when Duke is at the piano he is drumming the greatest . . . he has a wonderful touch . . . it's not noticed as much because, behind a solo, he's playing in the background where he's supposed to be—not in the foreground.' Yes, that was it, the Duke was a prodder, a solid rhythm man but always exercizing his imagination, a smoothly working pivot for the orchestra. Yet the phrases, the moods he produced exactly echoed his character—lazy, sporadic, imaginative, always inventing and composing on the spot, a minimum of histrionics, nothing merely braggardly (which was why we wondered that he put up with the Anderson squeals), always within the soulful orbit of the blues, the great jazz tradition, yet always adventuring. Ellington's struggle was always to keep the band going. 'We are not,' he said, 'one of those people who stay in the business only so long as business is good. We stay in it fifty-two weeks of the year.' Pressed in 1958 to give up the tremendous strain of all this playing and touring, he said: 'I'm much too impatient to do that. I have a fear of writing something and not being able to hear it right away. That's the worst thing that can happen to any artist. In fact, if the band hadn't always been there for me to try pieces on, I doubt if I'd have gotten nearly as much writing done as I have. This business of being just a composer isn't easy. Look at the hundreds of good composers who come out of the conservatoires every year, write hundreds of symphonies and never hear them played. I prefer being sure my music will be played and heard, and the best insurance is having one's own band around all the time.' The fund of common sense that was first noticed when he was just a venturesome youth who happened to know where he was going remained active.

The 1960s and that part of the 1970s that were granted to him were a cumulative grand tour. Ellington continued on the triumphal Ellington path, scattering his gems of genius, still indulging his sublime lapses of taste; always being himself, rightly creating what he thought fit to create and not what his critics thought he should, and by now everyone knew that nothing would change his course. He was simply a legend and the whole world wanted to see and hear him. He was to move into the grand-old-man of music period in the '70s,

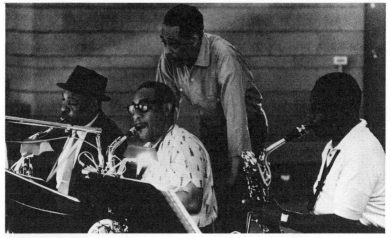

Duke Ellington at a 1962 recording session with (l to r) Coleman Hawkins, Johnny Hodges and Harry Carney.

revered in the way we tend to revere great conductors when they have gone through their periods of discredit and disgrace and we begin to appreciate the size of their individual contribution.

By now he could write what he wanted unchecked and have the most grandiose ideas. The list of works is impressive, especially for those who expect jazz to forget its plantation and bordello origins and enter the conservatoires. In 1960 there was *Suite Thursday* (Steinbeck inspired), and jazz versions of the *Nutcracker Suite* and *Peer Gynt*, plus music for the film *Paris Blues*. In 1962 there were recordings with Charlie Mingus and Max Roach; in 1963 he wrote a show for the Century of Negro Progress Exposition in Chicago called *My People,* and a *Timon of Athens Suite* for the Shakespeare Theatre at Stratford; in 1964 the *Far East Suite;* in 1965 the symphonic *The Golden Broom and the Green Apple;* in 1966 the first Sacred Concert seemed to indicate that a heavenly benediction had truly descended to carry him beyond the realms of the earthy jazz world; in 1968 the Second Sacred Concert; the Third came in 1973. These meant a great deal to Ellington. His deep religious feelings, instilled in him as a child by his beloved mother, never waned or weakened. 1970 had seen *The River,* a ballet for the American Ballet Company, and the *New Orleans Suite;* 1971 brought the *Togo Suite (Togo Brava).* In 1973 his fascinating autobiography *Music is my Mistress* appeared. At his end in 1974 he was working on an opera. The world simply sat by in bemused admiration or protesting conservatism. There was always the stick-in-the-mud cynic around who would trade all these prestigious works for the recordings of those unparalleled vintage years like 1940.

The Ellington cavalcade rolled on over these years. There were European tours in 1962, 1963, 1964, 1965 and 1967; of the Middle and Far East in 1963; Japan in 1964; Africa and Japan again in 1966; South America and Mexico in 1968; Eastern Europe in 1969; Russia in 1971; the Far East again in 1972. The ordinary mind boggles and the spirit wilts at even the thought of all this travelling, all those hotels and receptions, by a man well into his seventies.

In between were the high society occasions that gave Duke so much satisfaction, such as the famous 70th Birthday Party at the White House when he was presented with the Medal of Freedom by that paragon of Presidents, Richard Nixon. Forty years after his first appearance there, there was a Command Performance at the London Palladium. At the end of his autobiography fifteen pages are taken up by a list of the 'Honours and Awards' that he had received up to 1973 to press home the feeling that, with Duke Ellington, we are dealing with somebody who goes beyond the bounds of mere jazz and piano playing. The irony, of course, is that it is just those quintessential moments of jazz and piano playing, fleetingly caught on record fifty or more years ago, that are the nuggets that we seek and find in this awe-inspiring and arduous journey through life.

In May 1974 Ellington was fighting the lung cancer he now knew was hastening his end. Two close associates had recently died, Paul Gonsalves and Tyree Glenn, adding to the long list of people he had mourned and survived over the years—Joe Nanton, Bubber Miley, Johnny Hodges, Billy Strayhorn. We haven't said much about Strayhorn, the little *alter ego* who came into his life in 1939, did so much to colour his thoughts and his music, then died of cancer in 1967 taking a part of Duke with him; but he will come into the music. Ellington himself gave up the struggle on 24 May 1974. Among the mourners was Harry Carney experiencing the saddest day of his life (he was only seventeen when he joined the band in 1926 and had never left it, having become Duke's chauffeur as well as providing the pivot sound of the Ellington muse for nearly fifty years). Carney was himself to die in October.

In summary one can only feel and say that the total achievement of Duke Ellington, the music he wrote, the records he made, the impact he had upon millions of people, the legacy he left, is so large that anything said in a short essay is inclined to sound like a glib generalization. If we must hang on to one graspable facet it must be the music. In the souvenir programme for the 1958 tour Ellington wrote a piece called 'The Future of Jazz'. He went into the attack against diehards who believed that jazz was not supposed to be prepared or planned in any way, and went on to say:

'A theory they hold is that there is such a thing as unadulterated improvization without any preparation or anticipation. It is my firm belief that there never has been anybody who has blown two bars worth listening to who didn't have some idea about what he was going to play before he started. If you just ramble through the scales or play around chords, that's nothing more than musical exercises. Improvization really consists of picking out a device here and connecting it with a device there, changing the rhythm here and pausing there; there has to be some thought preceding each phrase that is played, otherwise it is meaningless.'

He concluded: 'I won't attempt to say whether the music of the future will be jazz or not jazz, whether it will merge or not merge with classical music. There are simply two kinds of music, good music and the other kind. Classical writers may try to write in the jazz idiom and the jazz writers may venture into classical territory, but the only yardstick by which the result should be judged is simply that of how it sounds. If it sounds good it's successful; if it doesn't it has failed.* And let's not worry about whether the result is jazz or this or that type of performance. Let's just say that what we're all trying to create, in one way or another, is American music'.

If, in sheer bulk of notes applied to paper, it seems far fetched to bracket Ellington as a composer with Mozart or Schubert, so be it. (He has been called 'The Hot Bach', but that doesn't mean very much either.) It was only a different way and a different sort of creation. He was not just writing notes for others to repeat and make significant. He was creating ideas that would lead musicians of the band into creating more, setting whole waves of creation into motion.

---

*'Whatever sounds right, is right'—*Robert Schumann.*

Progressive Gavotte:
ELLINGTON ON RECORD

1920s

Coming to the music, which must mean for the most part the recordings, the true individual Ellington sound seems to have manifested itself at the beginning of 1927. It was almost completely there in the 1926 *Immigration Blues* and *The Creeper* (the still earlier sequence of records he made for Gennett showed hardly a hint of it); but the full consummation is first revealed in the *East St. Louis Toodle-oo* recorded on 14 March 1927. This, with other recordings made that year, of titles that were to stay in the Ellington repertoire until the end, is a point where the jazz historian must inevitably hover for some time and try to analyze what made up the Ellington style and why it is so distinctive.

As a background to this it is interesting to reflect on what else was happening around March 1927. We are well past the pioneering days of recorded jazz and the distorted but energetic sounds of the Creole Jazz Band where Oliver and Louis Armstrong tried out the two-cornet breaks that were to take jazz away from the earthy simplicities of early New Orleans music. In April 1927 Oliver was leading a band in Chicago that had much the same makeup and intent as the current Ellington band, including in its ranks, beside such renowned players as Oliver himself, Kid Ory, Omer Simeon and Luis Russell, one of the future vital elements of the Ellington aggregation, the New Orleans clarinettist Barney Bigard. But the sound is simply that of a number of brilliant soloists doing their own thing held together by fairly straightforward arrangements (many of them by Russell) that varied in complexity but are organizational rather than imaginative.

29

A three man reed section gives the 'big band' feel. By this time Louis Armstrong was coming up to the classic Hot Seven sides with Ory and Johnny Dodds as front line partners. The Armstrong sound and style were well established. One could fruitlessly speculate on what might have happened if Armstrong had drifted into the Ellington band instead of into Fletcher Henderson's. Instinct, aided by hindsight, tells us that it was a mixture that would not have worked; a conclusion later confirmed on the few occasions when Ellington and Armstrong did get together.

Most importantly, perhaps, Jelly Roll Morton was at his peak with his Red Hot Peppers recordings. It must be assumed that, at some time Morton, in his indiscriminate way, had offended Ellington, for Duke makes very little mention of Morton and displayed an unusual lack of generosity towards him. In fact, Morton is the other great organizational talent at work at this time: the 'swing' pioneers like Fletcher Henderson had not yet fully got into their stride. There is a similar element of personal magic in these great Morton recordings as there is in the early Ellington releases; yet, while Morton comes through as an established piano stylist, his own contribution is the only element that is consistently flavoured. The rest is not so much the resourceful use of a number of good soloists as the exploitation and arrangement of the collective New Orleans sound. In historical terms Morton was then at a peak and most of what he did afterwards was a comparative decline. Ellington was to go on for five decades more, not consistently to any greater heights, but certainly in many fascinating experimental directions.

Within the three minutes or so of *East St. Louis Toodle-oo, Black and Tan Fantasy* and *Creole Love Call*, the germinal creations of 1927, lies the secret of Ellington's individuality, his genius, his method and his lasting power. Each piece has a slightly different aspect of his genius to reveal. Ellington's musical training had been fairly rudimentary and certainly most of his jazz knowledge was self-acquired by absorption from more or less obscure sources. He is known to have listened to the commercial music of the day and learnt from it some of the conventional devices of scoring and arrangement which he tended to use before his own unique powers had completely developed, enabling him to fill out a total canvas without recourse to common practice. While some people went to music schools to be taught how to compose and orchestrate, Duke Ellington had the sort of ability

30

that we find in Mozart and Schubert, the ability to sort out their own thing and to acquire certainty of touch from experience rather than instruction. He learnt to write the music he wanted to write by mentally filing what he heard, discarding what did not fit in with his personal tastes, developing what was to become a necessary element in his style. As reported by his son, Mercer Ellington, an early admirer with the unpromising name of Gump hit on the truth about Duke at the beginning of his career. 'He knew', said Gump, 'how to think'. While other jazz musicians were simply blowing their hearts out, Ellington was sitting back and considering. Morton was the other person who tended to do this, and we know more about what he thought because he never stopped talking about it. In the course of a strange autobiography, *Music is my Mistress*, Ellington adroitly manages to avoid telling us the truths we really want to know. He tells us of obscure piano players he listened to as a lad and comments that they all had their individual styles. But we remain in the dark as how they actually played, because none of them ever recorded. He was, as we have seen, a great admirer of James P Johnson and occasionally we can hear him doing a James P imitation on record in a slightly tongue-in-cheek sort of way. An educated guess might be that Willie 'The Lion' Smith was one of the people who mattered most in this respect. Certainly Ellington professed a supreme admiration for him. Smith's style was always more eccentric than the rest, more unpredictable and more imaginative.

While Ellington's orchestral style was certainly an echo of his own slightly eccentric, very personal and frequently under-rated piano style, the rest was to come from the musicians he used and, in the best sense, exploited. Now it might be considered very much the luck of the draw who he came into contact with and therefore used in the band, but there are hints, in his own writings and elsewhere, of a fairly deliberate choice-and-rejection process. That two such elements as Duke Ellington and Johnny Hodges should float into one another's orbit is either the greatest piece of good fortune or a supreme example of discrimination. Without Hodges one feels that many of the greatest things could not have been written. But those were days yet to come.

By the time he came to create and record the 1927 *East St. Louis Toodle-oo,* Ellington had already sorted out the elements on which he would like to build, and one senses that he was able to write for certain people because he understood them and he understood them because he liked them and they were in the band for that mixture of reasons. One of the first stable elements in the Ellington entourage, going back to the 1926 days of the Washingtonians, as the emergent band was first called, was Otto Hardwick, usually known as Toby. Playing the now archaic C-melody saxophone, Hardwick was a musician of comparative experience when Ellington got to know him. Duke loved the sweet, full tone that Toby drew out of his instrument, calling it, in his sidelong way, 'my first outstanding sound indentity'. The C-melody saxophone was quite familiar in the jazz and dance band world of the 1920s; Frankie Trumbauer played it with Paul Whiteman and used it on the classic records he made at the same time with Bix Beiderbecke. Hardwick was also one of the first to bring the baritone saxophone, his other main instrument (though he also played bass sax), into jazz and it was his playing of it that inspired Harry Carney to sound the first notes that led on to him becoming the greatest of them all on that instrument. Saxophonists at that time tended either towards slap-tongue comedy or saccharine sweetness; until Coleman Hawkins showed how the instrument should be played. It was the sweet sound that Ellington liked and Hardwick's legitimate tone, allied to a very resolute line, probably made Ellington feel that an integrated but decisive saxophone section was to be a personal part of his sound. Ellington has said, in his book, that he always wanted to base his big band, when it got going, on Fletcher Henderson's. It was, he says, the sound he wanted to achieve when he had enough musicians. In fact, one is inclined to disagree with Duke here, on listening to *East St. Louis Toodle-oo*. The reeds, Rudy Jackson on clarinet, Hardwick, and Carney leading with his likewise direct and hard hitting style, are already un-Hendersonian. If it is more relevant to say that the piece is built around the growling trumpet of Bubber Miley, the co-composer, it is the saxophone section that gives the piece its peculiar flavour starting with the long, curdled notes of the opening section which turn out to be a memorable counterpoint to Miley's solo which follows. The immediate juxtaposition of two themes may not be remarkable in itself, by classical standards or even in the world of improvized jazz; but in Ellington's hands both the 32-bar song theme that Miley handles and the accompanying theme are excellently crafted, cunningly subjoined to create a theatrical atmosphere that it is difficult

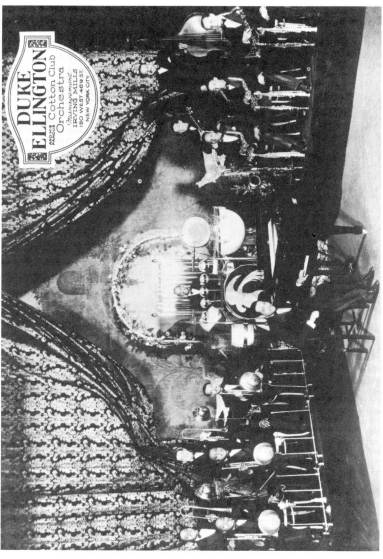

Duke's Cotton Club Orchestra in the late 1920's. (l to r, back row) Joe Nanton, Juan Tizol, Sonny Greer, Fred Guy, Wellman Braud. (l to r, front row) Freddy Jenkins, Cootie Williams, Arthur Whetsol, Harry Carney, Johnny Hodges and Barney Bigard.

to find anywhere else in jazz at this date. It is this theatricality, the sophistication, the love of smoothness that has often offended some jazz purists in Ellington's work; an offence that Morton, for example, would never give because his musicians, however ambitious his ideas for them, would always be playing in the essentially 'hot' idiom. The sombre quality of the opening is then sharply contrasted with a lighter, almost jaunty section, perhaps of less stature but at least demonstrating a sense of contrast rare in jazz recordings of the period where one mood per side was generally the order of the day. Billy Strayhorn later called all these things the 'Ellington effect', which again emphasizes the theatrical element in Duke's music—which is itself perhaps only a reflection of the theatricality of his life. *East St. Louis Toodle-oo* has a burlesque atmosphere about it, a nervy feel in many ways, with the jokey use of mutes, the lugubrious saxophones contrasting with Miley's vocalized playing. The rhythm becomes infectiously jocular with Nanton's vaudeville trombone setting a light mood which Hardwick suavely continues. The brass take up the song theme while the saxophones find a new one and the whole band piles in. As coda, Miley adds his last conversational comments against the original subdued counterpoint of the reeds. A simple formula, but one that takes the whole conception a step or two beyond the average jazz performance of that time.

The other two masterpieces of the year, compositions that Ellington was to use and re-use right through his career, are *Black and Tan Fantasy* and *Creole Love Call*. Between April and November 1927 he recorded *Black and Tan* three times (four if we count an unissued version), and each time it was in a different mood. The first, made on 7 April was light, delicate, even pensive over the explosive rhythm of the tuba; the second is strong and forcible with Wellman Braud added on string bass to give that propelling rhythm so typical of his work; the third, on 3 November, is odd and introverted as if Ellington was experimenting with the piece, as he no doubt was. Its form is similar to that of *East St. Louis*—a formal opening, a chordal section, a romping passage, all-in band and final coda. *Creole Love Call,* vitally different in its experiments with the wordless voice (Adelaide Hall) is still in this overall shape. Yet each of the three items has a strong individual personality.

Probably the key work is *Black and Tan Fantasy*. It sets the tone, in its varied exposition, for a whole range of subsequent Ellingtonia.

Most obviously it establishes the 'jungle' style, with growling and wa-wa muted brass that was to be a leading Ellington hallmark for the rest of time; secondly, it anticipates the subtle voicings which Duke projected, primarily via *Mood Indigo*: take the opening trumpet-trombone combination of *Black and Tan*, add a clarinet, adjust the balance, and you have the *Mood Indigo* voicing that was to be so prominent a feature of Ellingtonia up to the end. If the muted brass work looks forward to and through *Echoes of the Jungle* and *Ko-Ko*, and was to be the most immediately familiar Ducal 'sound' for more than four decades, the embryonic *Mood Indigo* voicings were to be, the more subtle and, it might be, insidious elements of the romantic Ellington productions in this complementary though no less indigenous Ellington style. It is easy to see that *Black and Tan* is itself a more or less embryonic Ellington composition. Its main theme is based on the old Stephen Adams ballad *The Holy City* which co-composer Bubber Miley's sister used to like to sing. The initial idea is strong and positive; but some of the working-out is less than that. What with the redundant piano solo, quite out of place in such a piece, and some conventionally scored ensemble passages, the main burden falls on Miley himself, and to a certain extent on Hardwick who provides the necessary contrast. Nanton's solo is again somewhat vaudevillian, as though Duke was still not sure what kind of music he was trying to create and what taste he was appealing to. But the fact remains, *Black and Tan* is the progenitor of virtually the entire Ellington creative world to come. It has also, besides the jungle and 'blue' connotations for later work, that haunted quality which is also an Ellington trademark and was first ennunciated in a contemporary composition, *The Mooche*. Like all men of a predominantly romantic disposition, Duke Ellington had a deep vein of melancholy running through the whole of himself and his creativity: if manifests itself as much in his 'jungle' music as in the more obvious 'indigo' strains.

The character of all these early pieces is set by the tone of Bubber Miley's trumpet. Often Miley is co-composer, or co-creator, and there is no doubt that his personal influence on Duke's early development was at least as potent as that of Hardwick in the 'sweet' department. The history of Bubber Miley and his evolution is interesting. He was not originally a 'growl' specialist. Garvin Bushell, who was his colleague in Mamie Smith's band in the early 1920s, recalled that what turned Miley in that direction was listening to

King Oliver when he and Miley heard Oliver together in Chicago. 'Before that Bubber never growled,' Bushell said. 'It was hearing Oliver that did it.' There is no doubt that Miley was primarily responsible for the evolution of the Ellington 'jungle' style, ably supported by Tricky Sam Nanton. To be strictly accurate, the first man to catch Duke's ear with the effect of muted brass sounds was trombonist Charlie Irvis, otherwise known as Charlie Plug, who preceeded Nanton in the trombone chair and worked his exotic effects by manipulating a broken mute in the bell of his instrument. But it was Miley who erected the growl and wa-wa technique into a leading musical principle. Although it is likely that the Ellington band's 'jungle' sounds helped them land and hold the job at the Cotton Club, it is a mistake and a critical solecism to see these muted brass techniques as merely freak 'effects'. If it had been no more than that, they would have passed into ephemeral history and soon been forgotten. To the contrary, they are, at their best, strictly musical devices, used by the Ellington men as techniques to emphasize and reinforce the melodic line. Indeed, Miley's great strength was his melodic gift, the quality of his melodic inventions. Allied to this gift for lyric melody, invariably blues inflected, Miley's subtle skill and sensitive deployment of the muted corollary was what primarily distinguished his own contributions and the overall character and quality of the Ellington productions during his tenure in the band. The most distinguished example of Miley's lyric gift allied to use of the mute and the 'growl' is to be found in his long solo on *Blues with a Feelin'* (Okeh, 20/11/1928). This, along with *Black and Tan*, is perhaps the ultimate testimony to Miley's melodic conceptions and power of expression. Often Miley's highly vocalized playing and his hard hitting phrases are couched in a rough, rather primitive vein. There is an animal quality about many of the recordings made while Miley was in what in the New Orleans days would have been the lead position. With Ellington he was asked to take his place with the rest but is still a dominant voice and his tone is the tone of the pieces. But in many moods, no one, not even Nanton later on, achieved the same subtlety and melodic sensitivity with the growl. His successor, Cootie Williams, already a marvellous player who adopted the Miley role (whether under orders or from his own assessment of his requirement) developed an even greater range, largely on account of his magnificent open playing. We have little evidence of Miley's open work, and virtually none at all how he played before he joined Ellington when he was a member of Mamie Smith's Jazz Hounds in company with Bushell and the teenage Coleman Hawkins; what is clear is that after he learnt the trick from King Oliver he seldom played open, at least in his Ellington days, but became the supreme musical master of the technique with mutes. A somewhat fey temperament and an increasing addiction to the bottle which hastened the ravages of the tuberculosis which brought about his premature death a few years later, caused his departure from the band early in 1929, and with his going Duke Ellington lost one of his original creative comrades and a basic source of inspiration.

The later recordings without Miley are a different thing altogether. Nanton is still inclined to sound mainly jolly in these early recordings, even his 'talking' trombone passages are slyly satirical. As the years went by he produced a deeper blues-tinged contribution. He came from Trinidad and much of his best work has a quality of West Indian jauntiness combined with an ominous deep-sound dramatic implication. None of his successors ever quite recreated this particular ambience. Several of them displayed considerable skill with a muted trombone style; but that was not the same thing at all. Tricky, like Bubber, was unique and irreplaceable.

These two, Nanton and Miley, helped to evolve the typical Ellington brass sound. Behind them the saxophone section already began to have what one might term a madrigal effect, the voices individual and independent within their harmony, rather than the close harmony effect that others like Fletcher Henderson seemed to be aiming for. The many-coloured contrapuntal sax section became even more distinctive as other musicians took over.

Barney Bigard joined the band in 1928, bringing a new mobility with his New Orleans style, Noone-like, clarinet sound, mellow but agile. And with Arthur Whetsol's poignant tone added again to the trumpets, there is now a new flavour to contrast with Miley's. The new, richer flavour can be savoured in such tracks as *Jubilee Stomp* and *Black Beauty* recorded on 21 March. When Johnny Hodges came into the band, from Chick Webb's, soon after, the saxophone section was enriched beyond measure; not to mention his supremely confident solos. Otto Hardwick, who was absent for a time but was back for the 1929 recordings, had, as we have already noted, a very basic saxophone tone and we soon hear a fascinating contrast between his legitimate sound and the wholly individual and unmistakable Hodges sound, the two flavours mingling with the equally recognizable qualities that Bigard and Carney were bringing to the clarinet and the baritone saxophone.

The more vivacious items of the period are counterbalanced by the reflective, nostalgic poetry of the blues orientated pieces like *Awful Sad,* and it is noticeable that Whetsol is made the dominant brass voice here. Such numbers are basically little but Ellington's highly individual piano style orchestrated. Of the 1929 *Hot and Bothered* Constant Lambert made those oft-quoted remarks: 'I know of nothing in Ravel so dextrous in treatment as the varied solos in the middle of the ebullient *Hot and Bothered* and nothing in Stravinsky more dynamic than the final section. The combination of themes at this moment is one of the most ingenious pieces of writing in modern music.'

Fair enough: but it is only right to recall that Gunther Schuller has pointed out that the performance sounds under-rehearsed and ill-prepared, with several false entries and some untidy ensemble work. The idea is fine, but the execution remains imperfect. Other versions of the piece concurrent with the famous Okeh recording are under characterized and far less exciting.

When we come to the confidently striding, insouciant pieces of mid-1929 we are instantly aware that the tones of Miley have been replaced by a voice no less vocal, no less earthy if less subtle, yet one with a new panache about it, a new swagger and a new smoothness. The trumpet of Cootie Williams has now become the leading voice in such pieces as *Ring Dem Bells* (on which he also 'scats' in duet with Hodges's alto) and *Saratoga Swing.* Now, whatever has been lost with Miley's going, there is a new top gear drive to the band and some exciting blends of three distinct trumpets played by Williams, Whetsol and the bright-toned Freddy Jenkins.

Thus by the end of 1929 three of the prominent Ellington solo voices for the next dozen years and more—Hodges, Williams and Bigard—were firmly established. Others, like Lawrence Brown and Rex Stewart were to come in later, and one, Joe Nanton, was already there; but the overall pattern was now set. The entry of Hodges into the ranks also brought back an old and pervasive influence, that of Sidney Bechet. Bechet had worked with Ellington briefly in 1924/25, soon after the band's arrival in New York. According to Bechet's own account, they made some good records which for some reason were

38

never issued and have disappeared. Johnny Hodges was Bechet's protégé, his only significant one. He occasionally played soprano sax as well as alto; he played it on the *Blues with a Feelin'* already mentioned. To the regret of many he did not resort to that instrument as often as they would have liked in later years, concentrating his great gifts on alto; but his presence in the band was a constant reminder of Bechet, and that influence was to pervade Ellington's music, subtly if not on the surface, until the end.

1930s

It might be instructive now to take note of some of the comments of Ellington's early critics. The *Melody Maker* in London took a keen interest in the doings of American bands in the late 1920s and 1930s. The British dance band scene was a thriving one but it relied on the jazz coming in from America to keep in fashion and make progress. Reviewing *East St. Louis Toodle-oo* and *Hop Head* (recorded in 1927) in September 1927, 'Needlepoint' (Edgar Jackson) said: 'While they have a red 'hot' peppy dance rhythm and are thoroughly bright and interesting there is not the musicianship behind these combinations which is found, for instance, in The Charleston Chasers. Two of the combinations [reviewed], Fletcher Henderson's and Duke Ellington's, are coloured bands, and while one must admit that our negro friends certainly go all out for it rhythmically, they are at times inclined to be rather crude.'

Reviewing *Take it Easy* and *Jubilee Stomp* (recorded January 1928) in the August issue of that year, 'Needlepoint' wrote: 'With perhaps the exception of Fletcher Henderson's *Whiteman Stomp* and a couple of others by the same band . . . the above are the best performances I have heard from a coloured band. Both compositions are by Duke Ellington himself. *Take it Easy* is typical of him. There is something extraordinarily appealing about it. The misunderstood soul of the whole negro race cries out from it. As regards performance, of course the band plays 'hot', and in doing so exhibits a much more up to date style as well as better balance, tone and ensemble than the usual run of coloured bands. There is some very surprising technique displayed by the various solo instruments—particularly in the saxophone which in *Jubilee Stomp*, a fast number, plays rapid passages in good modern style, with almost faultless execution. This is a record which will, of course, evoke the usual abuse from the Crowhard fraternity. Personally, I must admit, I get a greater thrill every time I play it. I live with these coloured folk through every bar of it. I appreciate, particularly in *Take it Easy*, their fight for serious expression, as I do their childish humour. It is a record with which, in spite of the fact that its best friend could not call either side a great musical work, I shall never part.'

A slightly condescending attitude to 'coloured' music was typical of the *Melody Maker* at that time. It was the records of Red Nichols and Miff Mole that were held up as models of good taste and proper jazz styling. Black music, to English tastes, still sounded a bit primitive. By 1931 'Mike' (Spike Hughes) was in charge and an altogether more informed musical appreciation was in evidence. Looking back to the great days of the Memphis Five, and listing some of the Ellington band, including such mis-spelt names as 'Joe Naunton' and 'Wellman Brand', 'Mike' tells how one record, *Creole Rhapsody*, was raved about by Major Christopher Stone, but he himself found it a little disappointing. He could not see it as a great piece of music although without doubt it was the most ambitious effort heard in England since *Washboard Blues*. The real Ellington masterpiece, he said, was *The Mooche*, not then easily available. *Creole Rhapsody*, he went on to argue, was not in the strict sense 'hot' music and it was far too sophisticated for the public which buys its records in bicycle shops. He hailed it as the 'first classic of modern dance music'. 'In spite of the obvious limits of a strict unvarying four-four rhythm . . . the Duke has created some moments of rare beauty—the principal theme, in particular, is sad and haunting.'

In October 1931, he said of *Wall Street Wail* that the tune was so good that all the band had to do was keep on playing it over and over in various combinations—and they did just that. In November 'Mike' found *Limehouse Blues* and *Echoes of the Jungle* the best sides ever made by the band. 'This arrangement of *Limehouse Blues* reveals Ellington in his topmost form. There are the fabulous rhythm and colour, beautifully played solos, and an ensemble which is at times the most

40

disheartening thing in the world, so perfect can it be.' The greatest records, he proclaims, by the greatest band in the world. 'The playing of the brass—five of them, mark you—and the sureness of the high trumpet phrases, are things to be listened to again and again. We come to some lovely alto playing by Johnny Hodges every note of which means something, and whose tone, attack and musical invention are things of beauty and a joy for ever.'

In February 1932, *The Mooche* arrived and 'Mike' still thought it 'a record in a thousand'. 'The greatness of this record, as opposed to the ordinary run of dance performances, lies undoubtedly in the composition. It has not the ambitious progressions of, for instance, Don Redman's *Chant of the Weed*, but it has more sense of form.' In March it was *The Mystery Song* that he found 'quite out of the ordinary . . . it will suit any mood, grave, gay, depressed or delighted.' In May it was *Black Beauty*. 'Though I never considered Ellington's band so polished an aggregation at the Cotton Club as it later became, the record has that distinctive atmosphere and finesse which has characterised the performances of the band ever since, five or six years ago, Edgar Jackson, writing in these columns, thought it "must be a nigger combination". It was a crack worth getting in.' He added: 'We have learned a lot since then . . .'

Of *Lazy Rhapsody* and *Blue Tune*, in July 1932, 'Mike' remarks: 'It always amazed me how year in and year out Ellington manages to produce compositions which should be numbered rightly as *Mood Indigo* numbers 1,2,3 and 4 etc., and yet continues to command our attention and interest.' So the Ellington band arrived in England in 1933 with *Melody Maker* readers well primed in Ellington appreciation.

Before moving on to some further highlights of Ellington's extensive recording career, it may be illuminating to follow one of his 'masterpieces' through those years. What better for that purpose than *Mood Indigo*, certainly one of his most famous creations and one he must have recorded dozens of times and must have played thousands. It was first recorded on 17 October 1930, titled on some issues *Dreamy Blues*). It emphasizes a problem in assessing the works of a long-active composer like Ellington who is both creator and virtually sole authentic performer of his compositions to find that this version is already a perfect little masterpiece; the solos beautifully balanced, the accompanying work inspired, especially Braud's bass part, the rhythm and tempo just right; and above all the blending of that unique sound of muted trumpet, muted trombone and clarinet which was to be established as one of Duke's major contributions to the sound of jazz, to the voicing of a true jazz instrumentation. This was marginally the fastest version. Within two months Ellington had two more attempts on record. Neither had the same gem-like perfection. It was then tried in big-band guise, but this lacks the magic of that first fine careless rapture. In saying that certain Ellington performances are not especially good, we speak, of course, by Ellington standards. In the course of making hundreds of recordings, often, even probably, when there was nothing special to say, there were naturally mediocre and uninspired performances judged by the highest capabilities of the band. Having produced a perfect creation like *Mood Indigo* we might be inclined to think that it was best to leave well alone and not attempt it again. But every creative artist has the right to experiment, indeed must experiment if he is to remain creative. Another Ellingtonian dilemma that arises from this same piece is the recurrent inclination on his part to expand, to produce longer pieces of jazz. In this world of musical snobbery it is inherently implied in much criticism that length and 'seriousness' are synonymous with worth. The three-minute or so pieces required and enforced by 78 rpm recording were, as it happens, ideal for jazz; nothing could go on too long and the point had to be made in the time allotted. When Ellington expanded *Mood Indigo* into the length of half an LP side in 1950, some of the spirit was right but merely to pad out the piece with extended solos, that rarely sustained the inspiration, was pointless. There were still later versions of *Mood Indigo* which actually sounded trite, for example when Shorty Baker took over the solo part in the 1957 'Solitude' album.

Ellington's own fancifully whimsical 'plot' for *Mood Indigo* was that of a little boy who loved a little girl and, although she also loved him, he was too shy to make the right advances. He touches his cap to her each time he passes by her window, but her mother puts a stop to this. Eventually, he doesn't pass by any more and the little girl is left only with her mood indigo. The original trumpeter, Arthur Whetsol, gently and sympathetically produced the 'great big ol' tears' sound suited to Ellington's whimsy, and which Duke loved. He claimed to have written the piece, based on a theme offered by Barney Bigard, in fifteen minutes. It is quintessential Ellington of the period, with melodic lines of deep simplicity moving over chromatic harmonies that, for their time, were very advanced, a real sweet-sour effect conveying a feeling of relaxed melancholy rarely equalled in music. It makes us inclined to believe that Ellington's simple story version was perhaps the right one.

We may find ourselves, if we are honest, in this constant state of frustration and disappointment as Ellington admirers, at his propensity too often for doing things worse rather than better, the inclination to over-arrange and expand, the tolerance with bad singers and drummers and screaming trumpeters. So much depended on the individual quality of so many different players that it could never be the best all the time; but then Ellington often seemed to give in to these circumstances, to take the easy way out when creativity calls for, as pianist Artur Schnabel once intimated, the taking of the line of most resistance. On the other hand, it is easy to adopt a purist attitude from the comfort of the critical armchair: for Ellington one of the main problems was always to keep the band together, to earn enough money on the road and in the halls and studios to pay the bills, and if that sometimes meant pleasing the paying customers rather than the purists, often by mutilating a valuable piece of his own work, we have only so much right to complain. No doubt he often, especially in the later years, made the worst of several possible worlds; no doubt his taste was fallible—but then people of exclusively good taste seldom produce work of real value, and if they do, very little of it. Ellington worked in the rough and tumble of the world, and it is and always has been a world too frequently pleased by and willing to pay for vulgarity, the spurious and the tenth rate.

For Ellington there were bad periods with certain record labels; while others seemed to provide the right ambience and atmosphere. At times and periods, the magic was there; the masterpieces occurred. Certainly critical demands and standards were and are high, for we knew that Ellington at his very best was the supreme master. At these times no more exciting jazz has ever been put on record.

The which-way-shall-we-go situation of the Ellington band of 1930 is reflected in the number of names it recorded for and under: in that very year alone, it was ten different labels. When on Victor (for which they were supposed to be recording 'exclusively'—which no doubt accounts for the pseudonyms elsewhere) they were Duke Ellington and his Orchestra. On Brunswick they were often billed as 'The Jungle Band'; on such varied labels as Perfect, Banner, Oriole,

Rex, Velvetone, Okeh and Odeon, they might be the Ten Blackberries or Mills' Ten Blackberries, the Harlem Hot Chocolates, the Harlem Footwarmers or the Memphis Hot Shots. The latter was the pseudonym under which, for instance, they recorded the classic *Rockin' in Rhythm* for Okeh in 1930. Based on a theme by Harry Carney, it became very popular as a background for show dancers. It seemed a very adventurous piece of music then with its changing rhythms and unusual harmonies, and all the bands wanted to play it. It became one of those standards that never actually got written down, but the band were still playing it, with very little change, except rather faster, right into the 1970s.

The 1930s were years of cumulative greatness, the band settling into the kind of driving unit that was to make it a major force in the Swing era. Tracks like *Double Check Stomp* have the perilous headlong quality of a train doing 100 mph. One is held in a thrall of breathless excitement. It is the other end of the scale from the 'exquisitely tired and four-in-the morning' (Constant Lambert) *Mood Indigo*. In *Creole Rhapsody*, as Spike Hughes noted, 'the individual player is, for the first time, subservient to the personality of the composer'. Hughes clearly had his doubts about the slight pretentiousness that was creeping in and was to voice these feelings strongly as the years went on; but Charles Fox later saw it as 'one of Ellington's finest and most completely integrated works and a landmark in his musical development'.   Clearly it was a giver of confidence that such things could be done, but the age of the LP was still distant and so, perhaps fortunately, jazz was not yet tempted into the game of filling half an hour with endless introverted solos.

Of the other sides recorded in 1931, *Echoes of the Jungle, It's a Glory* and *The Mystery Song* are outstanding examples of the Ellington art at that time.

Echoes of the Jungle is another perfect conception perfectly executed. Ellington only recorded it this once, and apparently never returned to it. Perhaps we should be grateful. The experience of *Mood Indigo* warns that the danger of Ellington interfering with and diminishing some of his finest work was real. *Echoes of the Jungle* is so masterful that no improvement on it is possible, and no attempt desirable. Duke must have played it many times in the Cotton Club and on the air; but it never seems to have entered the band's regular repertoire and never, no doubt to its advantage, became a vehicle for virtuoso

The Ellington band in 1933. Photo: Max Jones files.
(l to r, back row) Sonny Greer, Fred Guy (guitar), Wellman Braud. (middle row) Duke, Otto Hardwick, Harry Carney, Johnny Hodges (partly hidden). (front row) Cootie Williams, Fred Jenkins and Arthur Whetsol.

exhibitions. *The Mystery Song* on the other hand might have benefitted from further attention. As Gunther Schuller has pointed out, the first half is Ellington at his most original and haunting, but the second part is more or less conventional band music of no great value, an 'anticlimax'. Schuller rightly suggested that if Duke had returned to work out the second half in terms of the first, another unique Ellington masterpiece might have emerged. But this one too Duke left alone and neither re-recorded nor took into the 'book'.

In 1932 Lawrence Brown came into the band to be greeted with mild horror by Hughes and other critics who saw this as the first encroachment of the smart element into the ranks. But Ellington obviously liked the new voice and Brown was to be with him for nearly twenty years, and later to rejoin until the end after a period of absence in the 1950s and '60s. Brown's ideas, which were by no means all *schmaltz*—he could play 'hot' solos of incredible technical agility—fitted in perfectly with the maturing and evolving Ellington style. Ellington used to say that if he wanted a new man in the band, he hired anyone who happened to be on hand and available: he never sent across country for anyone. But that seems like another of Duke's little foibles, or conceits: the way he took in players who were exactly suited to his immediate needs was too apt to be entirely coincidental. The traditional critics in particular disliked the oily blandishments of Ellington's song-orientated works like *Sophisticated Lady* where the sweet-toners like Brown and Hardwick (now back on station) dominated. Hughes even took exception to the over use of the term 'sophisticated', a word we are still regularly tempted to use in comparing Ellington's work at any period beside the less devious counterparts.

Ellington made recordings of *Sophisticated Lady* in September 1932 and March 1933, but neither was issued. Eventually he managed to sneak it out as the 'B' side of a recording of the established hit *Stormy Weather* (already a Cotton Club favourite), in May 1933, and it soon caught on. Ellington took great personal pleasure in Brown's trombone styling and he and Hardwick worked out an alto saxophone solo that has become a permanent routine. The basic idea for the song was Hardwick's. It has been said that the 'sophisticated lady' in question was Florence Mills who died suddenly and tragically in 1927 a week after returning from a triumphal European tour; the same year that Ellington began his association with the Cotton Club. But

46

Ellington himself was rather more vague and, probably tongue-in-cheek, said it was dedicated to 'all lady school-teachers who travelled and learned and spent holidays in Europe'. When Mitchell Parish added words to the tune later he had a more romantic vision of a sad lady sitting around in a nightclub covered in diamonds remembering her lost love.' 'Wonderful words,' said Duke, 'but not entirely fitting my original conception.'

Another result of Lawrence Brown joining the band was that the trombones were now brought up to three and the total brass to six. This meant a considerable increase in tonal richness and in basic orchestral potentiality. Ellington was not slow to take advantage of this new flexibility. The trombone trio of Joe Nanton, master of the plunger muted style, Puerto Rican Juan Tizol with his valve trombone and latin American bias, and Lawrence Brown with his highly sophisticated approach and technique, was an unbeatable combination, both in ensemble and in variety of solo potential.

When Ellington arrived in England in 1933 he at first tended to overdo the *Sophisticated Lady* brand of music making. Laurie Lee found Ellington intensely disappointing; 'a prophet who continually debased himself'. But there were some exciting things in the 1933 lists— the beautifully intricate whirlwind of *Merry-go-round*, the smooth insouciance of *Drop Me Off at Harlem;* and it was fun to see what a swinging masterpiece Ellington could make of such unlikely material as the music-hall type song *In the Shade of the Old Apple Tree.*

Much of the disappointment with Ellington at this time was his tendency to play more and more popular songs and other non-Ellington material, even though all of it was given the full Ellington treatment. Again, a good deal of this was due to the economic necessity of appealing to popular taste. But not all, and Spike Hughes was right to admonish when reviewing a particularly naive record of some trashy tune that it was Ellington's job to play his own good music not other people's bad music. An austere requirement, no doubt; but one takes the point.

A kind of uncertainty now creeps into the recorded output and from 1934 to '36 there is a fallow, shifting kind of activity. 1935 was the time for another extended experiment—*Reminiscing in Tempo.* This caused him a considerable amount of trouble and brought heavy criticism. The death of his mother had turned his mind backwards and as he himself said, it became more and more full of the past. The critics were not impressed. Hughes, in England, found it a 'long, rambling monstrosity that is as dull as it is pretentious and meaningless,' and John Hammond in America made it the basis of an article entitled 'The Tragedy of Duke Ellington'. However, there were some more encouraging voices and more sensitive appreciations. In England the late Leonard Hibbs took the trouble to listen and try to understand. He ended by calling it, intelligently, 'a Lob's Wood of jazz'. It is full of mysteries and secrets. Today it is still discussed and sometimes understood. Max Harrison has observed that 'Ellington put some of the very best of himself into *Reminiscing in Tempo*.' Harrison, though elsewhere expressing doubts about Ellington's command of form in 'extended composition', also draws attention to the fact that it is in three parts not four, and that the impression that it is in four parts is due entirely to the exigencies of 78 rpm recording, where it had to be spread over four sides, an inaccuracy not corrected in the LP transfer. Perhaps this is one work which ought to have been re-recorded taking advantage of LP; but by then, no doubt, the impetus had gone.

Harrison argues that the lack of room for solos and individual expression in *Reminiscing in Tempo* was 'no way to keep a jazz band happy, and may well explain why this most fruitful path was not pursued.' Maybe; but another and perhaps more immediate reason was that the hostile reception accorded to this very personal and private work simply discouraged him from attempting further excursions in that direction, at least for the time being. Duke often tended to be bashful about his 'extended compositions', perhaps a hangover from the days when he really did believe that people were more interested in hearing the band's on stage antics and pyrotechnics than his best compositions. Whatever of that, and however much contemporary critics may have turned up their noses, Duke left ambitions of that kind either unrealized or unissued.

At the time of *Reminiscing in Tempo* Ellington was perhaps suffering from further doubts as to direction. The punchy directness of the successful bands of the Swing era, such as those led by Benny Goodman, was hardly the right direction for a composer of his quality. Old voices went, such as Arthur Whetsol, who left in 1937. But Rex Stewart and Cootie Williams were well equipped to lead the band into the age of Swing. The most interesting facet of the band's activities now was the small group work that gave everyone a chance to get to know the stuff the band's leading soloists were made of, and they seem to be an encapsulated sample of the best of the great Ellington years to come. In those days virtually every big band featured one or more small groups from within its ranks (or in the case of Goodman, by additions to it)—the 'band within a band' as it was then called. Ellington, typically, took a slightly different route; but the results were much the same.

With the addition of Jimmy Blanton's amazingly forward looking yet incredibly swinging bass sound—the bass used as a melody instrument as well as part of the 'rhythm section'—the band took on a new life; and Ben Webster gave new strength to the saxophone section—although it had enough power already with Hodges and Carney coming into their full maturity. The band's constitution was now four saxes and six or seven brass (according to circumstance and availability the trumpets were either three or four, usually three permanents); and that was how it was to remain until the end, again with additions or subtractions along the way as time and inclination prompted. The encouraging new voice of Billy Strayhorn at his elbow was also a new boost for Ellington's often over-strained resources. Some of the load could now be shared.

By this time several of Ellington's songs were already established and many more were soon to become so. Alec Wilder in his penetrating survey of the popular song is inclined to find Ellington's output in this direction unsatisfactory. With justification he does not see Duke as a producer of great songs in the Gershwin, Kern bracket simply because that magical blend of music and lyrics is never found. In fact, most of the songs are just very good and very catchy instrumental themes and it seems likely that many of them had the lyrics added to the music—which is always a hard way to do things. They certainly sound that way, and even quite talented lyric writers like Paul Webster are to be found struggling to provide a verbal equivalent to Ellington's intricate melody lines. Few of the lyrics are memorable beyond an opening phrase or two.

1940s

In 1940 we move into a world of incredible richness, possibly the peak in the whole of Ellington's and the band's history. The band itself, now sounding totally integrated, rides along above Blanton's bass in a truly well-oiled manner; and this seems to allow Ellington (with what degree of Strayhorn's co-operation we shall never fully know) to work out the most exquisite and genuinely creative ideas in a number of directions. If one track had to be picked out as the outstanding Ducal achievement of the period, it might well be *Concerto for Cootie*, surely one of the most perfectly balanced and totally memorable pieces of 'composed' jazz ever produced. Beside it, and of equal eminence, are ranged a whole series of peaks such as *Ko-Ko, Jack the Bear, Across the Track Blues, Bojangles, Portrait of Bert Williams* and many others, including the ebullient *Harlem Air-Shaft*. Any LP that contains the pick of the 1940 recordings is an infallible delight. And to add to this there were some of the most perfect small group sides ever made—*Day Dream, Good Queen Bess, Things Ain't What They Used To Be* (composed by Mercer Ellington) to follow in 1941. The entire concept was based on Jimmy Blanton whose talents were fully revealed in four duets he made with Duke in October.

After a year like that, any other would have to take second place. 1941 had offerings like the band's signature tune *Take the 'A' Train* (typical of Ellington that it should be a Billy Strayhorn number) and Ivie Anderson (the one singer really suited to the swinging years) introducing *I Got It Bad and That Ain't Good*. The scourge of TB took the inspired Blanton to his grave at the age of 24 in 1942. Although Cootie Williams left to join Benny Goodman in the latter part of 1940; Barney Bigard left in 1942 and Ben Webster went his way in 1943, those early war years, despite losses, produced a band that Raymond Horricks has described as having 'a lust for life; it hit harder musically, bit deeper emotionally and swung more animatedly as it performed than any Ellington band that preceded it.' Some might be inclined to add 'or followed it'; but then it depends on what you mean by 'swing'.

One critic at least has suggested that the Ellington band never really achieved the power of swing until Blanton joined in 1939. This is manifestly untrue, although after the acquisition of Blanton the rhythmic foundations became more complex and minatory (but that is not the same thing). One could instance any number of Ellington records from the 1930s which 'swung' formidably—*Jungle Nights in Harlem (1930)*, *Jazz Convulsions* (1929) and *In a Jam* (1936), for example, all of which swing memorably, at least according to the tenets of that time.

At this point it might be as well to attempt some sort of assessment of Ellington in the wider context of jazz as a whole. While there are admirers of Ellington who take all that he did without any disloyalty to his art, the extent of his creative life probably means that most people have a preference for certain aspects or periods of his work and find it difficult to appreciate others. In the widest of basic Ellingtonian terms, he was the leader of what is generally termed in jazz parlance a 'big band', although at its biggest it had less than twenty players, usually somewhere around the 15-17 mark. It is not expected that a group of this size will indulge in free improvisation; its work has to be arranged and its ideas foreseen. However, within the band there were always, as in the bands led by Count Basie, Jimmy Lunceford or Benny Goodman, talented and inspired soloists who could have been the stars of less controlled groups had they wished. This is well demonstrated in the small group sessions that were a rich feature of the contemporary Ellington output. In the big band context Ellington conceived vehicles for these soloists that, it might be fairly claimed, made their contributions to jazz history even more memorable and pointful than if they had simply committed improvized solos to posterity. This great 1940s period is full of unforgettable associations of man and music—Rex Stewart in *Portrait of Bert Williams*, Ben Webster in *Cotton Tail*, Johnny Hodges in *Never No Lament*, Cootie Williams in *Concerto for Cootie*. At this period too Duke was stretching jazz to limits it had never hitherto experienced. The 1930s had perpetrated the association of particular men with particular works—*Echoes of Harlem* (Cootie), *Clarinet Lament* (Bigard), *Yearning for Love* (Lawrence Brown); but now there was a new and enlarged dimension. At this period too the 'stretching process' entered new dimensions, after *Creole Rhapsody* and *Reminiscing in Tempo*—not so much in length as in musical 'density'. Raymond Horricks says of *Ko-Ko* that it was 'one of the most important events in all jazz composition . . . using such daring modulations and instrumental voicing, using contrapuntal and rhythmic effects to enlarge the drama . . . to produce one of the monumental events in jazz music.'

On the other hand, Duke Ellington time and time again demonstrated his loyalty to the adage he put into a song title, 'It Don't Mean a Thing if it Ain't Got That Swing' (recorded in 1932 and put across with conviction by Ivie Anderson), by showing over and over, up to this period, how much he valued and enjoyed the infectious pulse of a band with rhythmic drive, effortlessly achieved. All the big black bands went in for this sort of thing—Basie, Lunceford, Chick Webb. Of them all, the Ellington band, at its best, achieved the overall drive of an organized swing band while at the same time retaining the improvized independent feeling. The many who consider the early 1940s recordings to have reached a peak that Ellington never surpassed do so because it does seem at this stage that Duke had everything balanced and all things going right at the same time. He was retaining the early jazz spirit, swinging like mad, had the best soloists to do the job with him, and was producing some of his most imaginative ideas as a jazz composer—conceiving them within a style that remains imperishable. Throughout the rest of his band-leading history Ellington was to try to retain this balance between the pure jazz spirit and the imaginative probings of a composer, and it must seem to many that he was too often tempted into trying his most precarious experiments at times when he had not got the basically reliable band to help him in those years, often employing musicians young enough to be his grandchildren. Belonging to an early jazz generation himself, Duke must, in later years, have found it difficult to continue in the vein that he really, secretly, enjoyed. Sometimes it seems that he was trying too hard to remain 'with it', but fashion dictated this. All one can say in retrospect is that the work of the early 1940s will never stale while some of the later pretentious efforts were stale from the start. Or at least to those whose vision of Ellington is couched in 1940 terms. Those brought up on a diet of 1950s or 1960s jazz must necessarily see things in a different light.

There was a natural hiatus in 1942 when an AFM ban on recording came into force, and the band was not to get near a recording studio again until the end of 1944. By this time there was a new look to some sections of the band, notably the trumpets—Shelton Hemphill, Taft Jordan, and Cat Anderson joining Ray Nance. In December

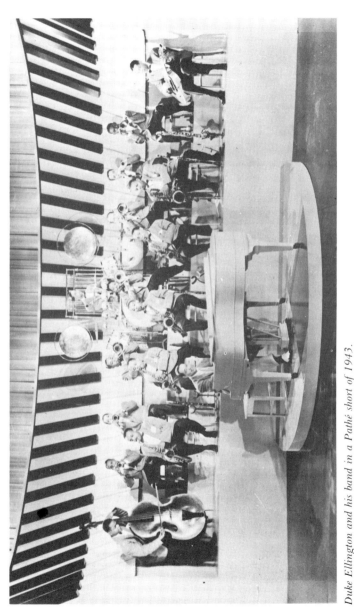

Duke Ellington and his band in a Pathé short of 1943.
(l to r) Junior Raglin, Ray Nance, Ben Webster, Wallace Jones (behind Webster), prob. Chauncey Haughton, Joe Nanton (behind), Jimmy Hamilton, prob. Sandy Williams, Sonny Greer (behind), Johnny Hodges, Juan Tizol, Harry Carney, Shorty Baker, poss. Taft Jordan, Fred Guy and Duke at the piano.

Ellington recorded his major work, *Black, Brown and Beige* suite. This 'Tone Parallel to the American Negro' is undoubtedly one of the works that will deserve, and get, future analysis when the academics get their teeth properly into jazz. It opens wider vistas for jazz, but also retains much of the early spontaneity and thus remains a thoroughly satisfying effort. *The Perfume Suite* of 1945 leans a little more towards the contrived regions. Another integral voice—and founder member of the band and its style—was wrenched from the Ellington conception when Tricky Sam Nanton died in 1946.

There is no room in this survey to look at all Ellington's recordings and compositions in detail, or even to list them. Therefore we must look at some more of the highlights of this staggering career. A brief flirtation with the Capitol label in 1945 held some indication of the generally unrewarding association that Ellington was to have here—though there were some exceptions. The Musicraft sessions of 1946, though frequently reissued, had some intriguing moments but little of the vital cohesion that produces great works. It was the return to Columbia in August 1947 that produced another superior succession of items that showed Ellington now ready to exploit some new voices in the band as effectively as he had handled the old ones—Tyree Glenn (tb, vib), Harold Baker (t), with Oscar Pettiford as a worthy successor to the Blanton legend, and the older hands maturing all the time, like good wines. In such titles as *Sultry Serenade, Golden Cress, Three Cent Stomp, The Clothed Woman,* Ellington produced some of his most subtle and effective compositions that rank among his best work, and the band, with Sonny Greer still there as anchor man, proves it can swing greatly and punch its way forward at the same time as it handles the delicate nuances of poetic subjects like *On A Turquoise Cloud, Lady of the Lavender Mist,* and Strayhorn's ambitious *Progressive Gavotte.* There is another piece from 1947 which has particular interest from several viewpoints. *New York City Blues,* shared almost exclusively between Ellington himself and Johnny Hodges, gives the immediate impression of an observer looking out over the city at night in a mood of ironic detachment. Musically, it is remarkable in showing how Ellington, like certain classical composers—notably the Chopin of the Mazurkas—could build a little tone poem out of a mere handful of notes. Here it is a tiny wisp of theme on which both Ellington and Hodges work—a mere three notes (four if you count the appogiatura) but which is made so evocative that an entire world of the fancy and imagination is built from it. This small and apparently unpretentious piece enshrines the quintessence of Ellington at this time.

1948 was bedevilled by another union recording ban and the Columbia association through 1949 produced no more masterpieces. This year also saw the band sinking into a trough. Tyree Glenn, a great trombonist, left, and the eventual departure of Sonny Greer would herald a succession of drummers who seemed unsatisfactory to anyone who revelled in the golden days of the 30s and 40s.

1950s

1950 was a year of general recession in the big band world. At the end of it Ellington was tempted into recording extended versions of *Mood Indigo, Sophisticated Lady* and *Solitude,* padding them out with a series of meandering solos that did nothing to enhance their already established qualities. And this was the last appearance of the great Johnny Hodges on an Ellington session until his return in 1955. He, Lawrence Brown and Sonny Greer sent a tremor of apprehension through the ranks of the Ellington fans and followers by defecting to the Norman Granz camp. It was a severe blow, a triple deprivation far surpassing the single one of Cootie Williams's departure in 1940. Duke had ridden that loss at a time when everything else was in the ascendant for him; but this new defection was something different. Hodges had become a leading, perhaps the leading voice in the band, and Brown, though a later acquisition to it had likewise become an important voice, even though disliked by many who could not forget the old days and early style, both solo and in the ensemble; and Sonny Greer was a genuine founder member who had been with Duke since his 'prentice days in Washington. Between them, these three had over seventy years of service in the Ellington cause.

1953 saw Ellington firmly associated with the Capitol label. He put a bold face on the shortcomings of this period, as he had to. He insisted that he still had a great band and a head full of ideas. He admitted that there was confusion abroad in the air, brought on by the 'bop' and 'progressive' jazz evolutions, not to mention the spate of 'revivalism' that had accompanied these new phenomena. The Capitol years at least produced the Ellington band in the new hi-fi of the LP era, and this often made some of the things more exciting. An LP entitled 'Ellington '55' caused quite a stir, but some of the music on it now seems rather static in certain respects, though it does contain one of his most memorable works—*Happy-Go-Lucky Local*, perhaps the most evocative tribute to his lifelong love of trains. An interesting bonus was an album with Ellington as soloist, and here one sensed him striving for that balanced effect which had produced his great moments. The band now was a big mechanical unit often turning out dreadful 'commercial' things like *Bunny Hop Mambo* and *Twelfth Street Rag-Mambo*, and endless albums, 45 rpm and LP, that asked us to 'Dance to the Music of Duke Ellington'. However much one may try to understand the motives and sympathize with him as he tried to keep the band in being at a time of huge financial stringency and against all the social and economic odds, this sort of thing was too sub-Ellington to last.

And of course it didn't. There was considerable disillusion in the Ellington fan club by now and something had to be done. Ellington did the right thing by quitting Capitol and going back to Columbia. This had always worked well before. Above all, Johnny Hodges returned.

To make up the loss of Hodges, Brown and Greer in 1951, Duke had gone out and purloined alto saxist Willie Smith, drummer Louis Bellson and his old comrade valve-trombonist Juan Tizol from the current Harry James band, in an operation that became known as 'the Great James Raid'. The infusion of new blood into the Ellington band was certainly welcome, even if it could never entirely compensate for the loss of the old hands. Bellson was, and remains, an outstanding drummer whose power served to re-animate the band at a time when it was showing distinct signs of staleness and ennui. Smith was a vigorous soloist, though far less imaginative and much coarser than Hodges; but he was a great section leader and he did much to pull the somewhat ragged Ellington saxophones together during the years of his tenure. Bellson contributed many fine performances and some highly usable numbers to the book, including the rather flashy *Skin Deep* and the potently swinging *The Hawk Talks*.

It was Bellson too who said later, in tribute to Duke, 'You Maestro, taught me not only to be a better musician but a better human being.'

It was ironic that the item that brought Ellington back into the popularity polls was a late night jam session during which Paul Gonsalves played 27 animalistic choruses and all the wonderful things that Duke could offer took second place to this rabble-rousing effort. There had even been doubts as to whether the Ellington band was right for a key place in the 1956 Newport Festival. Coming on late, many of the audience had begun to drift away when Gonsalves started on this bit of musical resurrection, interjecting his pyrotechnics between the two sections of *Diminuendo and Crescendo in Blue*. But that is the way things go in the entertainment world. It was, as Alun Morgan has said: 'a spontaneous triggering-off of emotions . . . not of great musical value.' None the less, it rebuilt the reputation of the Ellington orchestra. It gave Ellington the composer the courage for ambitious ideas again, one of which, an illustrated history of jazz called *A Drum Is a Woman*, a musically witty, tongue-in-cheek affair, brought choruses of disapproval from the critics. * It was criticized for all the things it did not do. They disregarded the wonderful writing for reeds, the exuberant work of Nance and Terry, the endless moments of pleasure and amusement. To balance this a paean of praise greeted Duke's next ambitious idea—a Shakespearean suite written for a Stratford, Ontario, dramatic festival. It was good that the jazz world in general recognized what Vic Bellerby called 'music of such restraint and thoughtfulness . . . with its sense of reserve and gentle enquiry into the Shakespearean characters.' It is a pity that such a large proportion of a potential musical and dramatic audience still cannot appreciate music cast in the jazz idiom, finding the rhythmic insistence a cheapening experience. For those who find it no objection the *Such Sweet Thunder* music would be a wonderful asset to the underlined scenes in the plays. In contrast to the products of a

---

* Writing in *Melody Maker* for 7 September 1957, Stanley Dance said: '"Jazz must have humour," says Duke Ellington. "I never heard of a really great jazz musician who didn't have a sense of humour." Duke is a really great jazz musician and *A Drum is a Woman* is full of humour. It seems necessary to stress first the element of humour, because "Pretentious" was the misplaced and misleading adjective common to several American reviews of this work.'

classical musical world where melody, in the sense that most people understand and appreciate it, is no longer written, *Such Sweet Thunder* is rich in 'inspired melody, long finely-shaped tunes . . . ageless in their beauty.' Indeed, Ellington's portrayal of Puck in 'Up and Down' bears comparison with Mendelssohn's *Midsummer Night's Dream* music. There is little in the whole realm of 'classical' music written to Shakespearean themes that is unquestionably more inventive than Ellington's. And it is genuinely related to Shakespeare. *

One critic praised the music but found a lack of completeness in the whole work. It certainly ended in an untidy way with the contrived and obviously unsatisfactory 'Circle of Fourths' which was simply Newport all over again. Perhaps *Such Sweet Thunder,* as many imply, was the apex of Ellington's composing. A sad reflection if it were indeed so, for he was still only three-fifths of the way through his active career.

An interesting LP of this period was one of two made for the small Bethlehem label in 1956. It is interesting because it again illustrates all those alarming contradictions that are a constant barrier to our uninhibited appreciation of Ellington. The record was called 'Historically Speaking' (and has since been re-titled several times in various reissues). It quite simply set out to re-create some of the best Ellington compositions in the light of his new band and modern LP recording. The sound was certainly impressive and it was indeed a band full of high class musicianship; and some items were impressively up-dated—for example, a *Creole Love Call* with some very juicy new harmonies added. One was impressed but slightly uneasy as it was realized that much of the old poetry of the original version had gone. Even worse—with some pieces it was sheer murder. Max Harrison called the recreation of *Ko-Ko* (long accepted as a perfect masterpiece) 'appalling . . . its essential qualities destroyed'. We remain unsure of Ellington's motives and criteria. Presumably he believed that he was improving matters, and of course there were always a few 'progressive' critics around to applaud such actions.

But perhaps after all it is not quite as simple as it seems. Max Harrison was not the only one to take exception to the 'recreated' *Ko-Ko.* Benny Green complained that the new tempo was some 25% faster than the old one, and so destroyed some of the atmosphere of

---

* See *Essays on Jazz* by Burnett James (London, 1962)

the original, opining that the old *Ko-Ko* was probably unimprovable anyway. All this, however, raises a point not usually considered. It is our habit, precisely because of their musical quality and relevance, to regard those old Victor recordings as definitive, if not as holy writ certainly as sacrosanct. But that ignores what Duke was doing at the time. If we listen to contemporary airshots, since issued on LP, we will often find that there were considerable differences, within 1940 itself and with the same band personnel, from the preserved performances in the Victor series; and this does not only apply to matters of tempo, although in the case of *Ko-Ko* the airshots show a notable increase in speed. It also applies to solo routines and the actual solos themselves. It is only since the release of these additional LP versions that we can make the proper comparative judgments and avoid that insidious trap from which critics frequently find it difficult to escape—the one-eyed view of what they decide they are considering. No doubt in the Victor studios, Ellington and the band thought they were doing their very best, and no doubt they were. We need not argue about that. But a piece of music, whatever it may be, is a living tissue and cannot be treated in performance as something fixed and static. If Duke saw his works of the past from a slightly different angle in his own contemporary present, that is only to be expected. He may have been right, or he may have been wrong; but at least he was not creatively mummified.

This does not of course mean that any or all of these 'recreations' supersede the originals; only that they represent a continuous and on-going attitude to music and its performance, which is necessary even if at times it appears decadent.

1960s/70s

From 1960 onwards, to take a rounded date, it would not be unduly harsh to say that Duke Ellington, more or less keeping step in age with the years of the century, was in his maturity. When that is said of a composer (and very often of a conductor or other performer) in the classical music world, we are almost automatically led to assume that we are moving into an area when his work, although it may lack some of the freshness and spontaneity of his early years, will have taken on a wisdom and depth that is the result of the rich insights garnered from experience. Most of the great composers (Mendelssohn is one of the few exceptions) have produced masterpieces at the end of their lives which stand among their finest, if not necessarily their most loved, achievements. Great musicians, until their physical powers and faculties fail, continue to add insight to their natural gifts. In the world of jazz, however, this rarely seems to happen. There is hardly a single major soloist who did not come to a peak in the middle of his career and then tend to fall away from it. Take an outstanding soloist like Louis Armstrong, a composer-performer like Morton; consider any of the big bands. It is the very nature and character of jazz that generally enforces this decline. Great jazz must have about it a natural freshness and spontaneity.

To write off the last decade or so of Ellington's career as a sad chapter of decline would be far from the truth. There were to be many glorious moments, times when the band could be relaxed and happy and swinging, times when the creative spark came back. And yet it is mainly true to say there was to be very little that was clearly better or even as good as the peak achievement of vintage years like 1940, 1947 and 1957. In jazz, indeed in any art, if you have once achieved perfection, what else is there to aim for? Once you have reached the top, the only way is down. Ellington admirers came away from concerts in the 1960s, or put aside new LPs of the period, so often with a feeling of disappointment. That word must crop up more often in reviews of the post-1960 years than with any other period. We were expecting to hear the miracles perpetuated. The wonderful Ellington sound was always there, the great soloists were with him almost to the end; but there was to be no new miracle. Soloists like Johnny Hodges retained their magic; but now they were like pop stars: people clapped delightedly just to hear that familiar sound in all its glory. But too often it was just a case of going through a tired routine.

To say this sort of thing is to risk the charge of fogeyism; but reviews of these years bear out that the Ellington devotee, while willing the maestro to produce his best again, was mostly obliged to come away empty handed. Writers of books on Ellington, Stanley Dance for instance, who knew Ellington better than anyone, tried to

60

Duke Ellington's first Sacred Concert, as performed in Coventry Cathedral in 1966.
Photo: David Redfern

maintain an enthusiasm for those later years; yet in an honest article in the American *Stereo Review* in 1969, Dance's approach suggests some doubts. The early and middle years are treated at length and with enthusiasm; the last few years are gone through with some haste. As the writings about Ellington, since his death, become more frank and revealing of his weakness and failures, we begin to have a feeling that these last years were, indeed, ones of mixed fortunes and inspiration. Ellington was able, of course, to bask in all the accumulated glory of his achievement. He was feted and honoured wherever he went. He received countless honorary degrees and his 70th birthday was celebrated by a party in the White House. He became more and more an ambassador for the American way of life and for his own black people. He was what the media call 'a legend in his lifetime'. But he must also have deeply felt the carping criticism, the lack of enthusiasm for his later music—and perhaps realized that it was inevitable. Like any good actor he kept up a front of cheerful optimism and an apparent belief that his latest work and his latest band really were the greatest. But he was probably very much aware within himself that the greatness upon which his reputation was founded was no longer in action. In saying this, one is not detracting from Ellington's overall achievement, but simply facing the undeniable facts. He produced the greatest jazz of all time, and some of the most original music of this century; and he was unshakably accepted as the greatest composer jazz had ever nurtured; a proven genius.

By 1960 the momentum of past achievement kept him and the band and his music in motion and demand. There was a long history of film appearances. In 1959 he had been commissioned to write the music for Otto Preminger's *Anatomy of a Murder* (in which he also appeared), and it won an award. Future commissions were to include *Paris Blues* in 1961, with a lightweight result, *Assault on a Queen* in 1965, and *Change of Mood* in 1969. None of these produced anything especially memorable.

The LPs continued to flow. By the late 1950s the critics had found that 'Bal Masque' and 'Ellington Jazz Party' 'enshrined a lot of very strange antics', like Johnny Hodges improvising on such unlikely materials as *Alice Blue Gown*, while *Ready Go* was yet another string of those repetitive Gonsalves choruses that since Newport 1956 had become all too prevalent. And Ellington himself often played in a style more reminiscent of Carmen Cavallaro than a thoroughbred jazz musician. There was a series of duet records with Hodges, but whether 'back to back', 'side by side' or 'face to face', they didn't really set the world alight and were sometimes supported by less than adequate rhythm sections. At this time Charles Fox categorized Ellington's piano playing as falling somewhere between Willie 'The Lion' Smith and Thelonious Monk—a not unsatisfactory position, although one he did not always maintain, being at times tempted into the cocktail lounge, or thereabouts. 'Festival Session'—another LP issued in the UK by Philips—had one or two ambitious but unsuccessful items like *Launching Pad*—a sort of *concerto grosso*. An LP entitled 'Blues in Orbit' was one of the most successful releases of this period with numbers such as the title tune and *Blues in Blueprint* 'inviting comparison with some of Ellington's most exquisite scoring of the past'. Jimmy Hamilton was one of the players who were allowed to help colour Ellington orchestrations. Around this time, when trombonist Matthew Gee occasionally played baritone-horn, the whole trombone section sometimes tried playing them, but this innovation was soon dropped. It was a period of uneasy experiments and the band trying hard to sound modern.

Next came some interesting but certainly odd ventures. Ellington and Strayhorn were persuaded to try their hands at a more ambitious way of 'jazzing the classics', that somewhat pernicious habit that has tempted jazzmen of all kinds and ages from the earliest days. The result was versions for 16-piece band of Tchaikovsky's *Nutcracker Suite* and Grieg's *Peer Gynt Suite*. On the whole the result with the *Nutcracker* was 'witty and stimulating' and often very effective; but the 'sheer awfulness of the *Peer Gynt* (as the *Gramophone* reviewer put it) probably made the *Suite Thursday* (with which it was originally coupled) seem better than it really is.' The Steinbeck-inspired *Suite Thursday* was originally coupled with the Grieg and the juxtaposition possibly caused some muddled thinking. One suspects a trace of musical snobbery, both ways, in the review quoted, although that critic made a shrewd, if somewhat obvious point when he went on to say that 'Ellington seems unable to develop his material to any great length.' The real point is perhaps not so much whether Ellington had the ability to 'develop' his material to great lengths as whether his particular material and his natural way of composing required that he should do so. In any case, such a criticism can be constantly levelled at jazz, at least on the superficial plane. Spontaneity is not a commodity that can be extended indefinitely, as many rambling jazz solos prove.

Some experiments that coupled Ellington with such 'progressive' musicians as John Coltrane, Max Roach and Charles Mingus must be accounted failures, despite some stimulating moments in the Roach/Mingus session. On the whole Duke Ellington did not fit in with such styles. He had his usual answer ready: when Mingus suggested they should do something 'really *avant garde*' together, Duke retorted, 'Oh, Charles, let's not go back *that* far'. He had done it all before; but the spirit of 'The Lion' was still strong in him. An album of piano solos called 'The Duke Plays Ellington' was a pleasant taste of his 'romantic approach to jazz'. A conglomeration called *The Symphonic Ellington* in which he was backed by various large orchestras was bound to be a 'disappointment', and inevitably it was. After all, there were and are many people who can compose for and competently conduct a symphony orchestra; but there was ever only one Duke Ellington.

What Stanley Dance accurately called 'Ellington's affinity with the theater' (in the face of everyone else's assertion that he never really found a niche in the 'musical') was tested in 1963 when he produced a spectacular show for the Century of Negro Progress Exposition in Chicago entitled *My People*. However effective this was on stage, the recorded result appeared 'lightweight . . . worthy but uninspired' to the *Gramophone* critic. Tours of the Middle East and India brought out the more interesting and worthwhile 'Far East Suite'—a collection of Ellington exotica. Tackling such unlikely material as *Mary Poppins*, Ellington achieved some not unpleasant results, but by now the critics were saying (with special reference to his recordings for the Reprise label, and even though one of these was the exploratory 'Afro Bossa') that it was 'time Duke gave us something worthwhile'. All that they got was an LP called 'Concert in the Virgin Islands', which was neither recorded at a concert nor in the Virgin Islands, and a re-recording of some of his old classics (mostly) in 'The Popular Duke Ellington' which showed how far he could stray from the great days by turning what had once been a succession of orchestral masterpieces into a string of tired solos over a swingless rhythm section. But this album too raises questions that need answering. On several tracks there is a touch of the old magic of the Ellington sound and the Ellington voicings which have never been repeated, let alone surpassed. On the other hand, there is rather too much evidence of another of Ellington's shortcomings—the willingness to take an older composition and turn it into a vehicle for some particularly favoured soloist of the moment. He did this a number of times with Paul Gonsalves; but perhaps his worst solecism in this respect was the way he turned *Harlem Air-Shaft*, one of the supreme masterpieces of 1940, into a vehicle for Clark Terry's flugelhorn. This particular outrage did not appear on 'The Popular Duke Ellington', but it was featured on at least one other LP of the 1960s and at several concerts. There was of course no reason why Duke should not have given the admirable Clark Terry an outing with his flugelhorn. What he should have done was to have written a new piece specifically for that purpose, not ruined an old one. One has the impression that Ellington both under-and over-rated his own compositions. He appeared to care so little for them that he did not hesitate to diminish and vulgarize them, no doubt under the pressures of keeping the band in being and in public favour; perhaps he actually thought they were so imperishable and unimpeachable that they would suffer no lasting harm whatever he did with them. In this sense again, some of the earlier masterpieces like *Echoes of the Jungle*, were fortunate that he never returned to them.

On the Verve label *Soul Call* proved to be a mixture of 'the very good and the pretty bad'. A new work for symphony orchestra *The Golden Broom and the Green Apple*, premiered at the Lincoln Center in 1965, proved to be Ellington in his most artifical vein.

It was a pleasure to welcome two LPs which came somewhere near to his best. *And his Mother called him Bill*, 'the most satisfying new Ellington LP for some time', was a tribute to Billy Strayhorn who had died in 1967. In the baldest terms Strayhorn might have been described as a musical assistant to Ellington. He had been taken on the payroll to help with routine orchestrations, but, as Fenby had been to Delius, Strayhorn became almost a part of Ellington himself. It will be difficult for the future historian to work out with any certainty what Ellington himself and what Strayhorn (or 'Swee' Pea' as he was always known) contributed to their innumerable joint productions or even to those under their individual names. At many concerts, and sometimes on recording sessions, Strayhorn would slip into the piano seat while Ellington directed, and their styles, though different, took on similarities that are sometimes difficult to separate.

Strayhorn's *Take the 'A' Train* had become the band's signature tune. His death was a great blow to Ellington and must have made his work all the harder. At the same time one wonders how much Strayhorn had helped push Ellington, with his younger and probably more advanced ideas, into ways that the older Ellington appreciator found less than satisfactory. It is all a matter of speculation, but the recorded tribute to Strayhorn found the Ellington band in that calm, relaxed, rhythmic mood that always seemed to suit it best.

And so it was too with the 'New Orleans Suite' which was hailed as 'among the most satisfying of Duke Ellington's latterday works' with one track, the reminiscent *Second Line* described as 'a small but authentic masterpiece'. Sidney Finkelstein had once written in his pioneering book, *Jazz: A People's Music,* that Ellington was responsible for 'restoring, within the narrow confines of a single band, the social character of New Orleans music', meaning that the atmosphere and opportunities that a stable band like Ellington's provided could give musicians the opportunity to create in the old New Orleans way. In this light, it was a pity that the suite could not include a tribute to Jelly Roll Morton, but the coolness towards that wayward genius remained until the end.

In 1968, after his tour of South America and Mexico, Ellington produced a 'Latin American Suite' which, while returning to a more artificial style, was full of clever impressionistic writing. His philosophy by now, as reported by Mercer Ellington, was 'you have to get away from your customary way of doing, and you have to do a lot of *forgetting.*'

Unfortunately, forgetting was just what the admirers and the critical fraternity could not and would not do. They were happy during the 1960s to be able to draw upon and write about a number of splendid LPs that brought back the old days and the old Ellington repertoire from the 1920s and 1930s on Decca's Ace of Hearts and Vocalion labels, in a scholarly series from Columbia (CBS) and from EMI on Parlophone. From the 1940s on, RCA's international catalogues boasted an *Intégrale* Ellington edition. With these and some smaller labels looking for obscurely recorded and broadcast material most of Ellington was to be found on some record or other, frequently in varying versions or in 'takes' not previously released. All these reissues were, of course, hailed with almost unqualified delight, particularly those from the great 1940s period. While the newer records were so often in the 'disappointing' category, at least to the older if not actually ageing among the faithful, the early ones now all became 'masterpieces' happily gilded by time. But this was not merely critical conservatism; at least not all of it. There really was some justice in it. The old tracks came back, and always will, as fresh as the day they were recorded. Much of the new sounded world-weary and many of those LPs of the 60s and 70s are now among the great unplayed.

Ellington found his consolation in paying tribute to his religion and his religious upbringing and beliefs in a series of Sacred Concerts. They may have brought him satisfaction and honour among the establishment of various countries but the musical only found them, however sincere (which they undoubtedly were), a curious mixture of the pretentious and the banal with a spicing of the Ellington magic breaking through all too occasionally. These and some concert recordings, including the last one at Eastbourne, were the ultimate products of those final years in which only 1968 and 1970 found some small peaks to alleviate the chagrin of the ever hopeful old customers.

In total, of course, his 50-year achievement was utterly remarkable, various and varied, up and down, but hardly ever less than distinctive and so often great beyond compare. At his best he was a Schubert of the jazz world. It was Miles Davis who said: 'Some day all the jazz musicians should get together in one place and go down on their knees and thank Duke.' As far as possible, together in the wide world of jazz, they did just that when Duke died in 1974. The feelings of all were finely captured in funeral orations delivered with great sincerity and sadness by Stanley Dance on 27 May 1974 in the Cathedral Church of St. John the Divine in New York, and by Derek Jewell in the Church of St. Martin-in-the-Fields in London on 12 June.

It was the end of an astonishing career; a life which had made the world a better place to live in. The jazz world to many seemed rather empty; but we soon got over the bereavement, as humans do, and cheered up at the thought of all the riches he had left behind for us to enjoy and analyse.

Lazy Duke
SUMMARY

The appellation was his own, c. 1930. It was not true, of course; he was not lazy; he was extremely industrious; it only seemed that he was 'lazy'; it was an impression he gave, by a kind of outward off-handedness, almost a form of apparent *je me'en fiche*ism in respect of both his own works and the music business in general. If discipline in the band was often ragged, the hand at the helm apparently undemanding, it was not because he was too idle to do anything else, still less because he didn't care: on the contrary, it was more nearly because he cared too much, had too high an opinion of his men to treat them to regular doses of his own authoritarianism. He ran himself and his band on a rein that was no less effective for being outwardly and apparently loose.

To take a less than idealistic view of jazz and Ellington, one less orientated towards a continuing line of development and a future for music, we can hardly underrate his actual achievement. Whether he should be summed up as a *petit-maître* of the musical world or a towering genius of the jazz scene, or a second line master of both has clearly not yet been decided. It is here that the estimates must vary widely according to personal taste and bias. Those who simply adore and praise everything that Ellington ever did have every right to do so. Those who hedge their bets have no less right and reason for their predilection. It is our ability to judge his sort of achievement rather than the achievement itself that is most suspect. One of the most perspicacious of writers on Ellington, Vic Bellerby, once made the rather surprising statement, having first criticized André Hodeir for dwelling too much on *Concerto for Cootie*, that it 'is fine, but not an Ellington masterpiece'. His basis for this assertion was that 'with a few strokes of the pen it was converted first into a popular ditty and then into a showcase for Lawrence Brown'. It is difficult to deduce which Bellerby thought most degrading. Surely by some reckonings, these, on the contrary, are valid reasons for a piece being rated as a masterpiece, a rating not to be evaluated only in terms of complexity or cleverness. Many of the greatest masterpieces of classical music are great precisely because of their simplicity and memorability—their popular accessibility, that is. It was a slightly snobbish outlook. *Concerto for Cootie* is an Ellington masterpiece, and one of the truly outstanding and indestructable moments of jazz. This does not in any sense mean a down-rating of other Ellington *oeuvres* that Bellerby prefers for their greater musical content or greater perception of an individual player's abilities—*Cootie's Concerto* (or *Echoes of Harlem* as it was additionally titled), *Barney's Concerto* (*Clarinet Lament*)—'listening to its superb progression serves as a reminder that Bigard was more difficult to replace than any Ellington musician'—and *Boy Meets Horn*—'a mixture of gentle wit and satire designed exactly for jazz's great sophisticate, Rex Stewart'. There is no need to run down any Ellington masterpiece to give others a chance. There are plenty of them. The one cause for regret is that Ellington could not go on producing them forever and nobody else has carried on the good work. But probably they have—in another idiom, style, period that Ellington himself could not belong to. That is for the modernists and the future to decide.

Jazz is essentially a lyric music. It has its baroque elements, its rococo and certainly its dramatic side. But at bottom it is a lyric form of expression. And from that it is a melodic music. And Duke Ellington, for all his harmonic adventurousness and rhythmic skill, was essentially a melodist. That is the main reason why his music tends to sound 'old fashioned'. Modern music, whether jazz or other, has tended to become more harmonic and textural than melodic, at least in the established and accepted sense, and for that reason among others has separated itself from the larger popular audience. In jazz, this process began with the 'bop' eruption of the early 1940s. It was not that the 'bop' musicians turned their back on melody; they did not. But by shifting the bias in improvization from the melodic to the chordal, they initiated a process which led to the subsequent

69

diminution of the role of melody, certainly of terminal melody which dominated European music, and therefore the European capacity for musical appreciation (which of course includes the appreciation of jazz), virtually from the time of Bach to the early years of this century. Inevitably, that particular melodic dominance lingered on beyond the time when in *avant garde* hands it has ceased to be either fashionable or even possible.

Ellington's propensity for reworking and representing his older compositions during the last years of his life was clearly linked to this. He composed melodic jazz when that form of music was in the ascendant; and when age and changing fashion touched him on the shoulder, he declined to chase the new devil by the tail. He continued to write and play the music he knew and understood and which was an authentic expression of his personality. He has not always been properly understood in this light. If some, particularly among the young, referred to him affectionately as 'Papa Duke' at the end, others either complained that he did not remain eternally young Duke or did not ally himself with all the 'progressive' notions of the up and coming young idea, forgetting perhaps that in the deep and real meaning of the term he had always been the most genuinely progressive of musicians.

Some of his later recreations of his early pieces were indeed rambling, diffuse and expendable. But not all. On the RCA album 'The Popular Duke Ellington', there is a new version of the 1928 *The Mooche* which is revealing. Inevitably, it is less structurally taut, less sharply focussed than the originals (it was recorded several times in 1928). And of course there is now (1967) no Bubber Miley and no Baby Cox. Yet anyone familiar with those originals will only need to hear a few bars of the later one to recognize instantly not just the voice and the voicings, but even more (and more significant) the eerie, haunted quality that made the piece always so memorable. The players may have changed, the arrangement revised and in certain respects enriched; but it is still Duke Ellington and it is still *The Mooche* and no one could fail to recognize it. The same is true of yet another version made a decade and a half earlier, in 1952, for CBS. Despite some contrary opinions and appearances, the inner continuity of Ellingtonia was sturdily preserved. The plain truth is and remains that Duke Ellington, whatever else may be said about him, produced, even when not at his very best, the most original,

Duke Ellington with Billy Strayhorn.

distinct and distinguished popular music of this century so far. And however you define popular music, between the extremes as it might be of Mantovani or Max Jaffa and The Beatles, or as it would be today 'hard rock', it remains the same; and it still remains if you pitch the definition anywhere in the hinterland between those far poles.

The greatest cause for regret lies in an area which touches on the snobbishness that intrudes into all music, including jazz. It is still wrong somehow that the general reference books which deal with so-called 'classical music', (the everyday catalogues and record lists rather than the new encyclopedias which seem to be more enlightened or have found it expedient to appear so and to include a few references to jazz and jazz musicians in their pages) can still find no place for Ellington. Sad but not altogether illogical. It is difficult to list Ellington as a composer when he left little behind that can be performed (something which Constant Lambert noted more than fifty years ago). That is why we have this imbalance between, let us say, Ellington and George Gershwin. Gershwin is listed because he left behind a piano concerto, a complete opera, many songs and other delicacies. In fact the juxtaposition of Ellington and Gershwin raises some interesting points and exposes some very muddled thinking. The Ellington obituary in *The Times* compared Ellington to Gershwin to the latter's disadvantage, apparently quite ignorant of the fact that the writer was committing the prime critical solecism of failing to compare like with like. Whatever may be said about Duke Ellington, past, present or future, invalid comparisons with other musicians, in whatever field, throw no light anywhere.

We can rate Ellington as a composer, in practical terms, only in the light of those works that he and his band left behind in recorded versions. It is a new concept of a composer, and one that the musical world still has to get used to and has so far found no convenient niche for classification. If it is true that it has sometimes been possible for other musicians to transcribe and convincingly recreate certain Ellington works, as Alan Cohen and Brian Priestley successfully did with *Black, Brown and Beige,* it remains generally true that the great majority of Ellington's compositions survive—apart from the simple tunes that have appeared as sheet music—only in his own performances of them. Most attempts to play Ellington by non-Ellington musicians are either travesties or simple straightforward improvization on themes. If Ellington had lived and worked before the age of recording, his music would not have survived beyond the occasions of its performance, certainly not beyond his own lifetime. It would have been and remained essentially ephemeral.

Ellington's second greatest legacy was, after his compositions (some might even be tempted to put it the other way round), the manner in which he led others into leaving behind supremely valuable and lasting contributions they might otherwise not have made— the work of Johnny Hodges comes immediately to mind, but a number of others are not far behind.

So far, no real justice has been done to Ellington. We have still to get our sights properly set on this great composer, musician and man. His life was a pivot for so many, close or distant, colleagues or admirers, good points and bad points regardless. Appreciation of his greatness will continue to grow and he must never be under-estimated.

Epilogue

I would like to add a personal note to end this otherwise mainly objective essay. Coming to jazz, as I and so many of my acquaintances did in the pre-war years, one then had to follow a tentative and haphazard path of discovery. Latching on to such titbits of information as were to be found in the fragile little magazines that were produced by pioneer gurus like Albert McCarthy and Leonard Hibbs (to whom we must acknowledge a great debt for their early perceptions), and in the very few books that had then appeared, most of which were to some degree biased, misinformed and only partly aware of what they discussed, we had to find our jazz in scattered crumbs, pecking around like sparrows in a hard winter. I first discerned the flavours of jazz in the bands of Ambrose, Lew Stone and Roy Fox (and in the trumpet of Nat Gonella) whose distant strains came through the earphones of my crystal set. It is easy to discern in hindsight that they drew much of their inspiration from Ellington. In a slightly more concentrated form I found it in the occasional Parlophone and Brunswick 78 rpm records by Red Nichols, Miff Mole and Eddie Lang and Pee Wee Russell that I came across. An even more concentrated essence was soon discovered in the likes of Louis and Bix and Dicky Wells. But jazz first really hit me, with all the potential magical intensity, when, one evening in Calcutta about 1946, an army educational jazz record recitalist (to whom I remain permanently indebted) played in his programme a couple of sides each by Jelly Roll Morton and Duke Ellington. From the first erratic genius we heard the strangely deep *Mournful Serenade* and the weirdly mournful *Deep Creek Blues;* and they were like a glimpse into a world of musical witchcraft, potent, primitive and strange; adding intriguing and fanciful literary flavours to the straightforward emotions of a simple jazz solo. These were followed by two no less strange tracks (strange that is to ears basically trained on the 'straight' music of the time) by Duke Ellington—*Creole Love Call* and *Black and Tan Fantasy*. Here was the same wild flavour that Morton offered but now it was being shaped and controlled and was much cleverer—yet no less potent. That evening my jazz tastes were formed for good.

Later after a decade of wallowing in Duke Ellington in the guiding company of Charles Fox and other jazz acquaintances, I was given the opportunity to edit a symposium on him. By the most fortunate and purest coincidence the book was completed and published the very week that the whole Duke Ellington band made a welcome return to England after a gap of a quarter of a century. On a totally unforgettable day I was able to present a copy of the book to Duke Ellington in person. It was a difficult act to perform because we met in the backroom of a London jazz club where we were so squashed together that it was even difficult to raise one's arms. In a room designed to hold about thirty people in comfort there appeared to be around three hundred. As Ellington was much taller than I am, my main vision of him was of the underside of the considerable bags that he wore beneath his eyes. He thanked me most courteously for having written a book about him, without showing any sign of being deeply moved, signed my copy, as he usually did, 'to my friend', handed his copy to an even larger man than himself (who appeared to be a sort of bodyguard) who made it disappear in the palm of his hand. The Duke then called upon no-one in particular, and with no visible response, to get me a drink. We were then swept on in different directions in the seething mob with a parting invitation from him to meet at his hotel during the week. I managed to chat in passing with a rather lugubrious Johnny Hodges; then with a contrastingly loquacious Billy Strayhorn who seemed ready to go on talking about Ellington and his music for ever. When I later met the Duke in the hotel lounge and in backrooms after concerts, he was always ready to talk shop, though he preferred not to, but, like most great composers, had very little of a revealing nature to say about his music. He never referred to the book and I don't know whether he read it or not. There were always too many people around, anyway, not to mention

The Duke in 1966. Photo: Val Wilmer

the 'stale cigarette smoke and the flat champagne', and he seemed as set on his refusal to talk about his genius as he was to waste time in quarrelling. He had the same attitude to business. He once said: 'Why should I knock myself out in an argument about fifteen dollars when in the time I can probably write a fifteen-hundred-dollar song?. . . I won't let these goddamn musicians upset me!' He tried not to let critics upset him as well, and he particularly didn't like having to answer all the same silly questions over and over again.

Some sixty years after he made his first tentative steps into jazz history and now, sadly, over a decade since he died, Duke Ellington's place as the foremost composer of jazz remains unchallenged. Already, in a world where change goes as quickly as you get it, where there is a mindless craze for the latest and supposedly greatest, it may be sensed that the music of Ellington is becoming a neat but vast parcel of historic material, due for some revival in the distant future like ragtime or music-hall. A critical problem is the vastness of his output and the fact that it covers so many periods and styles. To revive ragtime was simple because it was one thing. The music of Duke Ellington is many. The time has gone to write of the Ellington world in such romantic terms as: 'Pretty scents were another mass addiction of the Ellington musicians. There were always one or two bottles of expensive Paris perfume on Sonny's table, Sweepea (Strayhorn) went in for light, fresh odours, while Hodges experimented with colognes that would smell good when poured over small, coloured electric light bulbs', though I still find Danny Halperin's observations on Ellington, 'Everything Has to Prove Something,' * hilarious and moving. But there has been plenty of that sort of thing, even from the Duke himself; and we now know, to the point of boredom, that the band had rarified and expensive tastes that went with the more highly scented titles they recorded. I have a feeling, anyway, that the *Transblucency* and *Passion Flower* side of the Ellington output, was probably the most fleeting. It may be a bit conservative to say that we had the best of Ellington in the 30s and 40s, but there does seem to be a magnetic strength to the works of that period. Jazz musicians don't as a rule get better as they get older; they are more like athletes than their counterparts in the classical field, for vitality is all in jazz.

There is a true need to look at Ellington as we look at Mozart or Schubert; as a composer. It will need a big book one day, and I believe that at least a couple will soon be forthcoming. Perhaps we could make a start by giving him something approaching the nature of K (Koechel) or Opus numbers. It always seems to give a composer respectability. Then again, maybe not. Whatever line develops, there is still a lot of talk about Ellington to come. The present book, judged by these needs, is only a passing conversation.

---

* Reproduced in *Duke Ellington: his life and music* (London 1958)

The Ellington Sidemen

There has not been space in this limited volume to give detailed consideration to the many musicians who worked with Ellington over the years. We cannot overlook their importance as the instruments of his imagination. Some of them were passing thoughts but some of them were essential to his creative world. Ellington without Bubber Miley or Joe Nanton, Johnny Hodges or Cootie Williams would not be unthinkable but we would now be without some of his most treasured ideas. The following listing of the principal musicians who played and recorded with Ellington gives (in rounded brackets) the dates of the musicians where we have been able to ascertain them and (in square brackets) the dates when the player was with the band.

ALLEN, Charlie (1908-1972) [1935]   *trumpet*
ALVIS, Hayes (1907-1972) [1935-38]   *bass*
ANDERSON, Ivie (1905-1949) [1931-42]   *vocal*
ANDERSON, William 'Cat' (1916-81) [1944-47, 1950-59,
                              1961-71]   *trumpet*
ASHBY, Harold (1925-   ) [1968-74]   *tenor saxophone, clarinet*

BACON, Louis (1904-1967) [1933-34]   *trumpet*
BAILEY, Ozzie (1925-   ) [1957-58∞   *vocal*
BAKER, Harold (1913-1966) [1938, 1942-44, 1946-52,
                              1957-63]   *trumpet*
BALLARD, Butch (1917-   ) [1950, 1953]   *drums*

BASCOMB, Wilbur (1916-1972) [1947]   *trumpet*
BELL, Aaron, (1922-   ) [1960-62]   *bass*
BELLSON, Louie, (1924-   ) [1951-53, 1965-66]   *drums*
BENJAMIN, Joe (1919-1974) [1951-1974]   *bass*
BIGARD, Barney (1906-1980) [1927-42]   *clarinet, tenor saxophone*
BLACK, Dave (1928-   ) [1953-55]   *drums*
BLANTON, Jimmy (1918-1942) [1939-41]   *bass*
BRAUD, Wellman, (1891-1966) [1927-35, 1944, 1961]   *bass*
BROWN, Hillard (1913-   ) [1944]   *drums*
BROWN, Lawrence (1907-   ) [1932-51, 1960-70]   *trombone*
BYAS, Don (1912-1972) [1950]   *tenor saxophone*

CARNEY, Harry (1910-1974) [1927-74]   *baritone sax, etc., clarinet*
CASTLEMAN, Jeff (1946-   ) [1967-69]   *bass*
COOK, Willie (1923-   ) [1951-57, 1960-68]   *trumpet*
COOPER, Buster (1929-   ) [1962-69]   *trombone*
COOPER, Harry (1903-1961) [1926]   *trumpet*

DAVIS, Kay (1920-   ) [1948-50]   *vocal*
DAVIS, 'Wild' Bill (1918-   ) [1969-74]   *arranger, organ*
DE PARIS, Wilbur (1900-1973) [1945-47]   *trombone*

EDWARDS, Henry 'Bass' (1898-1965) [1925-26]   *tuba, bass*
ELLINGTON, Edward Kennedy 'Duke' (1899-1974)   *piano*
ELLINGTON, Mercer (1919-   ) [1964-74]   *trumpet, horn, arranger*
ERICSON, Rolf (1927-   )   *trumpet*

GASKIN, Victor (1934-   ) [1969-70]   *bass*
GEE, Matthew (1925-   ) [1959-60]   *trombone, baritone*
GLENN, Tyree (1912-1974) [1947-51, 1971   *trombone*
GONSALVES, Paul (1920-1974) [1950-74]   *tenor saxophone*
GREER, Sonny (1895-1982) [1920-51]   *drums*
GRISSOM, Jimmy (-   )   *vocal*
GUY, Fred (1897-1971) [1925-49]   *banjo, guitar*

HALL, Adelaide (1904-   ) [1927]   *vocal*
HAMILTON, Jimmy (1917-   ) [1943-68]   *clarinet, tenor saxophone*
HARDWICK, Otto 'Toby' (1904-1970) [1920-1928, 1932-1946]
                                              clarinet, saxophone

HAUGHTON, Chauncey (1909-   ) [1942-43]
clarinet, alto & soprano saxophone
HEMPHILL, Shelton (1906-1959) [1944-49]   *trumpet*
HENDERSON, Rick (1928-   ) [1953-55]   *alto saxophone*
HIBBLER, Al (1915-   ) [1943-51]   *vocal*
HODGES, Johnny (1907-1970) [1928-51, 1955-70]
clarinet, alto saxophone

IRVIS, Charlie (1899-1939) [1924-26]   *trombone*

JACKSON, Quentin (1909-1976) [1948-59, 1963]   *trombone*
JACKSON, Rudy (1901-1968) [1926-27]   *clarinet*
JEFFERSON, Hilton (1903-1968) [1952-53]   *alto saxophone*
JENKINS, Freddy (1906-1978) [1928-34, 1937-38]   *trumpet*
JOHNSON, Harold 'Money' (1918-1978) [1968-69, 1970-71] *trumpet*
JONES, Claude (1901-1962) [1944-48, 1951]   *trombone*
JONES, Herbie (1938-   ) [1963-68]   *trumpet*
JONES, Rufus (1928-   ) [1966-72]   *drums*
JONES, Wallace (1906-1983) [1938-44]   *trumpet*
JORDAN, Taft (1915-1981) [1943-47]   *trumpet*

KILLIAN, Al (1916-1950) [1948-50]   *trumpet*

MARSHALL, Wendell (1920-   ) [1948-54]   *bass*
METCALF, Louis (1905-1981) [1926-28]   *trumpet*
MILEY, James 'Bubber' (1903-1932) [1924-29]   *trumpet*
MILLS, Irving (1894-   ) [1927-1939]   *vocal, manager*
MINERVE, Harold (1922-   ) [1970-74]   *alto, clarinet, flute*

NANCE, Ray (1913-1976) [1940-44, 1945-63, 1965-71]
violin, trumpet
NANTON, Joe 'Tricky Sam' (1904-1946) [1926-46]   *trombone*

PETTIFORD, Oscar (1922-1960) [1945-48]   *bass*
PROCOPE, Russell (1908-1981) [1946-74]   *clarinet, alto saxophone*

RAGLIN, Alvin 'Junior' (1917-1955) [1941-44, 1946-47, 1955] *bass*
ROBINSON, Prince (1902-1960) [1925-26]   *clarinet, tenor saxophone*
RODNEY, Red (1927-   )   *trumpet*

ROYAL, Ernie (1921-) [1950]   *trumpet*

SANDERS, John (1934-) [1954-60]   *trombone*
SEARS, Al (1910-) [1944-49, 1950-51]   *tenor saxophone*
SHERRILL, Joya (1927-) [1944-48, 1956]   *vocal*
SMITH, Willie (1910-1967) [1951-2]   *alto saxophone*
STEWART, Rex (1907-1967) [1934-43, 1943-45]   *cornet*
STRAYHORN, Billy (1915-1967) [1939-67]   *piano, arranger*

TAYLOR, Billy (1906-) [1935-40]   *bass*
TERRY, Clark (1920-) [1951-59   *trumpet*
TIZOL, Juan (1900-1984) [1929-44, 1951-53, 1960]   *valve trombone*
TROTMAN, Lloyd (1923-) [1945]   *bass*
TURNEY, Norris (1921-) [1968-72]   *flute, saxophone*

WEBSTER, Ben (1909-1973) [1935, 1936, 1940-43, 1948-49]

tenor saxophone
WHETSOL, Arthur (1905-1940) [1920-23, 1928-37]   *trumpet*
WHITE, Harry (1898-1962) [1929]   *trombone*
WILLIAMS, Cootie (1910-1985) [1929-40, 1962-74]   *trumpet*
WILLIAMS, Elmer (1905-1962)   *clarinet, tenor saxophone*
WILLIAMS, Francis (1910-1983) [1945-1949, 1951]   *trumpet*
WILLIAMS, Nelson 'Cadillac' (1917-1973) [1949-51]   *trumpet*
WOOD, Mitchell 'Bootie' (1919-) [1959-63]   *trombone*
WOODE, Jimmy (1928-) [1955-59]   *bass*
WOODMAN, Britt (1920-) [1951-60]   *trombone*
WOODYARD, Sam (1925-) [1955-65]   *drums*

Bibliography

(a) **Biographical & Critical Studies**

THE WORLD OF DUKE ELLINGTON by Stanley Dance. New York: Scribners, 1970. London: Macmillan, 1971.

MUSIC IS MY MISTRESS: AN AUTOBIOGRAPHY by Duke Ellington. New York: Doubleday, 1973. London: Allen, 1974. New York: Da Capo, 1976. London: Quartet (pb), 1977.

DUKE ELLINGTON IN PERSON: AN INTIMATE MEMOIR by Mercer Ellington & Stanley Dance. Boston: Houghton Mifflin, 1978. London: Hutchinson, 1978.

DUKE ELLINGTON: HIS LIFE AND MUSIC edited by Peter Gammond. London: Phoenix House, 1958. New York: Roy Publishers, 1958. London: Jazz Book Club, 1959. Munich: Nymphenburger, 1961. New York: Da Capo, 1977.

PORTRAIT OF ELLINGTON by Don George. New York: 1982; London: Robson, 1983.

CELEBRATING THE DUKE by Ralph Gleason. Boston: Little Brown, 1975.

DUKE: A PORTRAIT OF DUKE ELLINGTON by Derek Jewell. London: Elm Tree Books, 1977. London: Sphere (pb), 1978.

DUKE ELLINGTON by G E Lambert. London: Cassell, 1959. New York: Barnes, 1961.

DUKE ELLINGTON, KING OF JAZZ by Elizabeth Rider Montgomery (for younger readers). Champaign, Ill: Garrard, 1972.

MOOD INDIGO by Denis Preston. Egham: Citizens Press, 1946.

DUKE ELLINGTON: SEIN LEBEN, SEINE MUSIK, SEINE SCHALL-PLATTEN by Hans Ruland. Gauting-Buchendorf: Oreos, 1985.

DUKE ELLINGTON: HARLEM ARISTOCRAT OF JAZZ by Jean de Trazegnis. Brussels: Hot Club de Belgique, 1946.

DUKE ELLINGTON by Barry Ulanov. New York: Creative Age Press, 1946. Buenos Aires: Editorial Estuardo, 1946. London: Musicians Press, 1947. New York: Da Capo, 1975.

(b) Music

PIANO METHOD FOR BLUES by Duke Ellington. New York: Robbins, 1943.

THE GREAT MUSIC OF DUKE ELLINGTON edited by Leonard Feather & others. New York & London: Belwin Mills, 1973.

(c) Discography

THE "WAX WORKS" OF DUKE ELLINGTON: AN UP-TO-DATE DISCOGRAPHY by Benny H Aasland. Stockholm: Aasland, 1954.

DUKE ELLINGTON ON MICROGROOVE, 1923-1942 by Dick M Bakker. Alphen aan den Rijn: Micrography, 1974.

JAZZ DIRECTORY, Vol. 3—E,F,G by Dave Carey & Albert McCarthy. Fordingbridge: Delphic Press/London: Cassell, 1951.

TWENTY YEARS OF THE DUKE, Part 1: 1933-1953 by Donald Russell Connor & others. Carnegie, Penn: Pope's Records, 1966.

DISCOGRAPHY OF DUKE ELLINGTON (3 VOLS) by Jørgen Grunnet Jepsen. Brande: Debut Records, 1959-60.

DUKE ELLINGTON'S STORY ON RECORDS (VOLS. 1-10) edited by Luciano Massigli, Liborio Pusateri & Giovanni M Volonté. Milan: Musica Jazz/London: Seago, 1966-75.

GENERAL CATALOG OF DUKE ELLINGTON'S RECORDED MUSIC by Luigi Sanfilippo. Palermo: Centro Studi, 1964 & 1976.

THE DIRECTORY OF DUKE ELLINGTON'S RECORDINGS by Jerry Valburn. New York: P.O. Box 156, Hichsville. (No date).

ELLINGTONIA: THE RECORDED MUSIC OF DUKE ELLINGTON by W.E. Timmer. Montreal: 1979

Obviously no Ellington enthusiast would want to be without Ellington's own point-settling autobiography *Music is My Mistress*, even though it does not settle as many points as the dedicated researcher might wish. It reveals much of the character and attitudes of the man but it is not logically put together, nor can it (except in a useful list of written works) be considered a reference work. The most ordered biography is Derek Jewell's *Duke*, romantically inclined but very readable and giving a well-rounded portrait of Ellington.

Further insights from his son Mercer are to be found in *Duke Ellington in Person;* while the flavour of the band at work and sketches of many of its principal musicians is the important part of Stanley Dance's *The World of Duke Ellington.* The older books could obviously only give a partial coverage of his life but both Ulanov and Lambert have valuable comments to make on his early music. *Duke Ellington: his Life and Music* includes some worthwhile essays such as Boyer's 'The Hot Bach' (reprinted from the *New Yorker*) and Charles Fox's excellent study of the 1930 recordings (which is also reprinted in Williams's *The Art of Jazz* (New York: Oxford University Press). The multi-volume Italian discography looks like being the definitive one. Publication is eagerly awaited of a detailed study of Ellington's recordings by G E Lambert; while several scholarly books on his music are also in preparation. It is to be hoped that the not too distant future will see a comprehensive and balanced work on Ellington that can be accepted as the standard one.

To the above should be added various essays and chapters that have appeared in general books and anthologies. Of prime import- ance is Gunther Schuller's study 'The Ellington Style' in his *Early Jazz* (Oxford University Press, 1968) also to be found in a slightly different form in *Jazz* edited by Nat Hentoff & Albert McCarthy (New York: Rinehart, 1959; London: Cassell, 1960; Quartet (pb), 1977). Although confined to the 1920s and 1930s, Schuller's analysis, with plenty of musical examples, of the Ellington method and style is a welcome introduction to the complete understanding of his genius, seeing this period as the laying of foundations. A thorough analysis of one Ellington work, the unsurpassed *Concerto for Cootie,* is to be found in André Hodeir's *Jazz: its Evolution and Essence* (New York: Grove Press, 1956; London: Secker & Warburg, 1956; etc). As many have done, he rates it as a masterpiece for its purity and positiveness, its rich musical substance where 'nothing is out of place or superfluous'. Only *Ko-Ko,* he says, can compare with it in the Ellington output. Constant Lambert's early appreciation of Ellington is oft-quoted and some of it is to be found in his *Music Ho!* (London: Faber, 1934 & reprints); though what he wrote has led to the continuing fallacy that Ellington was inspired by composers such as Debussy, Ravel and Delius. There is no evidence that he listened to a note of them. Some of Ellington's own rich badinage is to be found in the conversational anthology *Hear Me Talkin' To Ya* edited by Nat Shapiro and Nat

Hentoff (New York: Rinehart, 1955 and London: Davies 1955; etc).

Useful introductory pieces on Ellington (the earlier ones with historical interest in step with their dates) are 'Duke Ellington' by Wilder Hobson (written as early as 1933) in *Frontiers of Jazz* edited by Ralph de Toledano (New York: Durrell, 1957; London: Jazz Book Club, 1966); 'Duke Ellington' in *The Jazz Makers* edited by Shapiro & Hentoff (New York: Rinehart, 1957); 'I Let a Song Go Out of My Heart' by Stanley Dance in *The Decca Book of Jazz* edited by Peter Gammond (London: Muller, 1958); 'Duke Ellington' in *From Satchmo to Miles* by Leonard Feather (New York: Stein & Day, 1972; London: Quartet, 1974); 'Duke Ellington—Apex of the Big Band Tradition' in *Big Band Jazz* by Albert McCarthy (London: Barrie & Jenkins, 1974) 'Form beyond Form' in *The Jazz Tradition* by Martin Williams (New York: Oxford University Press, 1970, (pb) 1983); and, of course, in many more general histories and surveys. Of more specialised interest: 'The Ellington Programme' by Barry Ulanov in *This is Jazz* edited by Ken Williamson (London: Newnes, 1961); 'Johnny Hodges', 'The Impressionism of Duke Ellington' & 'Such Sweet Thunder' in *Essays on Jazz* by Burnett James (London: Sidgwick & Jackson, 1962); 'Reflections on Some of Duke Ellington's Longer Works' by Max Harrison in *Jazz Retrospect* (Newton Abbot: David & Charles, 1976; Boston: Crescendo, 1976). A general record survey is to be found in *Music on Record 2: Big Bands* edited by Peter Gammond & Raymond Horricks (Cambridge: Stephens, 1981); and some interesting records are thoroughly reviewed in *The Essential Jazz Records: Ragtime to Swing, Vol. 1* by Max Harrison, Charles Fox and Eric Thacker (London: Mansell, 1984).

Personal views of Ellington by his own musicians (except those reported by Dance and others) are not easy to come by as not many of them were addicted to writing. Of special interest, therefore, are Rex Stewart's reflections in *Jazz Masters of the Thirties* (New York: Macmillan, 1972; repr. Da Capo Press, 1982). Under the collective heading of 'Ellingtonia' he offers pieces entitled 'The Days with Duke', 'Sketches in a Ducal Vein', 'Duke Ellington: One of a Kind', 'Tribute to Tricky Sam', 'Illustrious Barney Bigard', 'The Frog and Me' (Ben Webster), 'Harry Carney: Boss Baritone' and 'Getting to Europe—and Getting Out'. An illuminating Ellington anthology. A recent addition is *With Louis and the Duke* by Barney Bigard (London: Macmillan, 1985).

Discography

To attempt a complete Ellington discography at all has become a formidable task, covering as it does almost 50 years of incessant recording and broadcasting. In a volume of this scope the best we can hope to be is wisely selective; but even that is not possible, for no solution to the problem would suit everyone in this fickle world of jazz. From the 1920s to c.1952 the tracks were recorded as individual items for issue as 78 rpm discs. Here we have tried to include the most important items and have attempted to indicate where they could be found on LP. Even this is not always practical for, as any serious collector will know, record companies have a way of putting things in and out of the catalogue with maddening disregard to the buyer's needs. In some form or other, however, two big projects have remained reasonably stable—the *Intégrale* series of issues from French RCA, edited by Jean-Paul Guiter, (which became available in five boxed sets as DUKE 1 (original Vols. 1-5); DUKE 2 (Vols. 6-10); DUKE 3 (Vols. 11-15); DUKE 4 (Vols. 16-20); DUKE 5 (Vols. 21-24), the single items having been withdrawn); re-issued as double LPs 'The Indispensable Duke Ellington' – 5 double LPs in 10 volumes; and the equivalent CBS 'Collected Ellington' made up of material from Columbia. Even here, as some of the later areas get covered, some of the earlier discs have been frustratingly withdrawn. The serious jazz collector is not going to be deterred by such matters. After 1952 the recordings were mainly designed for LP issue and this does simplify things. If, in common with the previous text, there is a tendency to emphasise the early material in this discography, this is intentional, as it is clearly in the more miscellaneous world of the 78 recordings that collecting interest lies. And the most essential music. Anyone who possesses the basic material that we have listed will be well served. Five times the amount then awaits the truly enthusiastic collector who has the spirit and cash to go further. It must be remembered, too, that not all the essential Ellington was put on wax in recording studio conditions. The band was continually on the road and giving concerts and broadcasts. A multitude of small specialist labels now offer a great deal of this material. Some of it, at least, should be heard to understand how much a performance could change in such circumstances.

I am grateful to Tony Middleton for his assistance in the preparation of this discography.

Labels (LP):— Atl = Atlantic; BBA = Big Band Archive; Cap = Capitol; CBS; CC = Collectors' Classics; Col = Columbia; Cor = Coral; Dec = Decca; HMV = His Master's Voice; JA = Jazz Archive; Lon = London; Par = Parlophone; Ph = Philips; Que = Queen; RCA = RCA Victor; Swa = Swaggie; Tax = Tax; UA = United Artists; Ver = Verve; Voc = Vocalion; Vog = Vogue; VJM = Vintage Jazz; WRC = World Records; etc.
Countries of Origin:— A = USA; B = Belgium; Aus = Australia; F = France; G = Germany; D = Denmark; J = Japan; Swe = Sweden; Swi = Switzerland. Those without prefix originate in Great Britain or are universal.

1926

Bubber Miley, Louis Metcalf (tp); Joe Nanton (tb); Otto Hardwick, Harry Carney, Rudy Jackson (reeds); Duke Ellington (p); Fred Guy (bjo); Bass Edwards (tu); Sonny Greer (d). *New York, November 29, 1926*

E4110	EAST ST. LOUIS TOODLE–OO	Dec AH166; Voc VLP4; Aus. Swa 111;
	(Ellington; Miley)	F.MCA 510101; A. Dec DL9224; VJM VLP71
E4114	BIRMINGHAM BREAKDOWN	Dec AH166; Voc VLP4;
	(Ellington)	VJM VLP71; Aus. Swa 111;
		F.MCA 510101; A. Dec DL9224

As above. *New York, December 29, 1926*

E4321	IMMIGRATION BLUES (Ellington)	Dec AH47; Voc VLP4; Aus. Swa 111;
		F.MCA 510011; A. Dec DL9224, 79241; VJM VLP71
E4323	THE CREEPER (Ellington)	Dec AH47; Voc VLP4
		(also incl. E4324); VJM VLP71
		Aus. Swa 111; F.MCA 510011; A. Dec DL9224; 79241

1927

As above. *New York, February 3, 1927*

| E4510 | NEW ORLEANS LOWDOWN | Voc VLP4; A. Dec DL9224; |
| | (Ellington) | F.MCA510011; VJM VLP71 |

| E4511 | SONG OF THE COTTON FIELD
(Ellington) | Dec AH47; Voc VLP4; VJM VLP71
F.MCA510011; A. Dec DL9224, 79241 |

As above.   *New York, February 28, 1927*

| E21641 | BIRMINGHAM BREAKDOWN
(Ellington) | Dec AH23; Voc VLP4; VJM VLP71
F.MCA510011; A. Dec DL9224 |

As above.   *New York, March 14, 1927*

| E21872 | EAST ST. LOUIS TOODLE-OO
(Ellington; Miley) | Dec AH23, Voc. VLP4; VJM VLP71
F.MCA510011; A. Dec DL9224 |

As above.   *New York, March 22, 1927*

143705	EAST ST. LOUIS TOODLE–OO (Ellington; Miley)	CBS 67264, A.Col C3L27; VJM VLP71
143706	HOP HEAD (Ellington)	CBS 67264, A.Col C3L27; VJM VLP71
143707	DOWN IN OUR ALLEY BLUES (Ellington)	CBS 67264, 66302 A.Col C3L27, C3L-39; VJM VLP72

As above.   *New York, April 7, 1927*

| E4874 | BLACK AND TAN FANTASY
(Miley; Ellington) | Dec AH23; Voc VLP4; VJM VLP72
F.MCA510011 A. Dec. DL9224 |

As above, except Wellman Braud (b) replaces Edwards. Adelaide Hall (voc).

New York, October, 26, 1927

39370	CREOLE LOVE CALL (Ellington; Miley; Jackson)	F.RCA 731043; RCA RD8089; A. RCA LPV568; PM43687; VJM VLP72
39371	THE BLUES I LOVE TO SING (Ellington; Miley)	F.RCA 731043; PM43687; RCA RD8089; A.RCA LPV568; VJM VLP72
40155	BLACK AND TAN FANTASY (Miley; Ellington)	F.RCA 731043; RCA; PM43687, RD8089; A. RCA LPV568; VJM VLP72
40156	WASHINGTON WOBBLE (Ellington)	F.RCA 731043; RCA RD8089; A RCA; LPV568, PM43687; VJM VLP72

As above, except Jabbo Smith (tp) replaces Miley.   *New York, November 3, 1927*

81775	WHAT CAN A POOR FELLOW DO? (Meyers; Schoebel)	CBS 67264, Aus. Swa 1234; WRC SHB58; VLP72
81776	BLACK AND TAN FANTASY (Miley; Ellington)	CBS 67264, Aus. Swa 1234; WRC SHB58; VLP72
81777	CHICAGO STOMP DOWN (Johnson; Creamer)	WRC SHB58; VLP72

As above, except that Bubber Miley (tp) replaces Smith.

New York, December 19, 1927

41244	HARLEM RIVER QUIVER (BROWN BERRIES) (McHugh; Healy; Fields)	F.RCA731043; RCA RD8089; A. RCA LPV568, PM43687; VJM VLP72 (2 takes)
41245	EAST ST. LOUIS TOODLE—OO (Ellington; Miley)	R.RCA 731043; RCA RD8089; A. RCA LPV568, PM43687; VJM VLP72
41246	BLUE BUBBLES (Ellington; Miley)	F.RCA 731043; RCA PM43687; VJM VLP72

As above.   *New York, December 29, 1927*
E6824   RED HOT BAND (McHugh; Healy;   Dec AH47; Voc VLP4; F.MCA
    Fields)   511011; A. Dec DL9224, 79241; VJM VLP73
E6826   DOIN' THE FROG (McHugh;   Dec AH47; Voc VLP4; F.MCA
    Healy; Fields)   511011; A. Dec DL9224, 79241; VJM VLP73

                                   1928
As above, except that Barney Bigard (clt) replaces Jackson.
                                                               New York, January 9, 1928
145488   SWEET MAMA (Rose; Little; Frost)   WRC SHB58; VJM VLP73
145489   STACK O'LEE BLUES (Lopez; Caldwell)   WRC SHB58; VJM VLP73
145490   BUGLE CALL RAG (Pettis; Mills; Schoebel) WRC SHB58; VJM VLP73

As above.   *New York, January 19, 1928*
400030   TAKE IT EASY (Ellington)   CBS 67264; 66302 VJM VLP9, VLP73;
                                          Aus. Swa 1234, WRC SHB58; A.Col C3L-3
400031   JUBILEE STOMP (Ellington)   CBS 67264, VJM VLP9, VLP73; Aus.
                                                     Swa 1234, WRC SHB58
400032   HARLEM TWIST (EAST ST. LOUIS)   WRC SHB58; VJM VLP73
    (Ellington; Miley)

As above, with Arthur Whetsol (tp) added.   *New York, March 21, 1928*
E27089   TAKE IT EASY (Ellington)   Dec AH89; Voc VLP4;
                                                             F.MCA510011
E27091   JUBILEE STOMP (Ellington)   Dec AH47; Voc VLP4,
                                                   F.MCA510011, A.Dec 72941
E27093   BLACK BEAUTY (Ellington)   Dec AH89; F.MCA510011; VJM VLP73

As above.   *New York, March 26, 1928*
43502   BLACK BEAUTY (Ellington)   F.RCA 731043, RCA RD8089; PM43687
                                            A.RCA LPV568; VJM VLP73
43503   JUBILEE STOMP (Ellington)   F.RCA 731043; RCA RD8089;
                                            A.RCA LPV568, PM43687; VJM VLP73
43504   GOT EVERYTHING BUT YOU (Palmer; Razaf)   F.RCA 741028; PM43687
                                            RCA RD8089, A.RCA LPV 568

As above, except that Johnny Hodges (a-s) replaces Hardwick.
                                                               New York, June 5, 1928
E27771   YELLOW DOG BLUES (Handy) Dec AH166, F.MCA510011; VJM VLP73
E27772   TISHOMINGO BLUES (S. Williams)   Dec AH166; F.MCA510011;
                                                             VJM VLP73

As above.   *New York, July 10, 1928*
400859   DIGA DIGA DOO (McHugh; Fields)   WRC SHB58; VJM VLP73
400860   DOIN' THE NEW LOW—DOWN (McHugh; Fields) WRC SHB58; VJM VLP73

Duke Ellington (p).   *New York, October 1, 1928*
401172   BLACK BEAUTY (Ellington)   CBS 67264; Aus. Swa 1231
                                                    WRC SHB58; VJM VLP73

| 401173 | SWAMPY RIVER (Ellington) | CBS 67264; Aus. Swa 123; WRC SHB58; VJM VLP73 |

As above with Lonnie Johnson (g) & Baby Cox (voc). *New York, October 1, 1928*

401175	THE MOOCHE (Ellington; Mills)	CBS 67264, Aus. Swa 1234, WRC SHB58; VJM VLP73
401176	MOVE OVER (Ellington)	CBS 67264, Aus. Swa 1234, WRC SHB58
401177	HOT AND BOTHERED (Ellington)	CBS 67264, Aus. Swa 1234, WRC SHB58

As above with Johnson & Cox. *New York, October 17, 1928*

| E28359 | THE MOOCHE (Ellington; Mills) | F.MCA 510017 |
| E28360 | LOUISIANA (Schafer; Johnson) | F.MCA 510017, Dec AH89, A. Dec DL9245 |

As above. *New York, October 20, 1928*

| E28441 | AWFUL SAD (Ellington) | F.MCA 510017, Dec AH166 |

As above except unknown tp (possibly Jenkins) replaces Metcalfe. Baby Cox (voc). *New York, October 30, 1928*

| 47799 | THE MOOCHE (Ellington; Mills) | F.RCA 741028, RCA RD8089, A. RCA LPV568; PM43687 |
| 48103 | NO, PAPA, NO (Spivey) | F.RCA 741028, RCA RD8089, A. RCA LPV568 |

Arthur Whetsol, Bubber Miley, Freddy Jenkins (tp); Joe Nanton (tb); Johnny Hodges, Otto Hardwick, Harry Carney, Barney Bigard (reeds); Duke Ellington (p); Fred Guy (bjo), Wellman Braud (b); Sonny Greer (d). Ozzie Ware & Irving Mills (voc). *New York, November 15, 1928*

48166	BANDANNA BABIES (McHugh; Fields)	RCA RD8089, A.RCA LPV568, F.RCA741028
48167	DIGA DIGA DOO (McHugh; Fields)	RCA RD8089, A. RCA LPV568, F.RCA741028
48168	I MUST HAVE THAT MAN (McHugh; Fields)	RCA RD8089, A.RCA LPV568, F.RCA741028

As above, without Hardwick but with Lonnie Johnson (g) added. *New York, November 20, 1928*

401350	THE BLUES WITH A FEELIN' (Ellington)	CBS 68275, Aus. Swa 1234, WRC SHB58
401351	GOIN' TO TOWN (Ellington)	WRC SHB58
401352	MISTY MORNING (Whetsol; Ellington)	CBS 68275, Aus. Swa 1234, WRC SHB58

1929

As above, with Hardwick, without Lonnie Johnson. *New York, January 8, 1929*

| E28939 | DOIN' THE VOOM VOOM (Miley; Ellington) | Dec AH23, F.MCA 510017 |
| E28940/1 | TIGER RAG (LaRocca) | Dec AH89, F.MCA 510017, A. Dec DL9245 |

89

As above, but without Hardwick.   *New York, January 16, 1929*
49652   FLAMING YOUTH (Ellington)   F.RCA 741028, RCA RD8089,
                                                   PM43687; A.RCA LPV568
49653   SATURDAY NIGHT FUNCTION   RCA PM43687; F.RCA 741028
           (Bigard; Ellington)
49654   HIGH LIFE (Ellington)   RCA PM43687; F.RCA 741028
49655   DOIN' THE VOOM VOOM (Miley;   RCA PM43687; F.RCA 741028
           Ellington)

Arthur Whetsol, Cootie Williams, Freddy Jenkins (tp); Joe Nanton (tb); Johnny
Hodges, Harry Carney, Barney Bigard (reeds); Duke Ellington (p); Fred Guy (bjo);
Wellman Braud (b); Sonny Greer (d).   *New York, March 1, 1929*
E29381   RENT PARTY BLUES (Ellington; Hodges)   Dec AH23, F.MCA 510017
E29382   PADUCAH (Redman)   Dec AH23, F.MCA 510017
E29383   HARLEM FLAT BLUES (Ellington)   Dec AH23, F.MCA 510017

As above.   *New York, March 7, 1929*
49767   THE DICTY GLIDE (Ellington)F.RCA 741029 (Takes 1&2); RCA PM43687
49768   HOT FEET (McHugh; Fields)   F.RCA 741029, Camden
                                                   CDN119, A.RCA CAL459; PM43687
49769   SLOPPY JOE (Bigard)   F.RCA 741029(Takes 1 & 2); RCA PM43687
49770   STEVEDORE STOMP (Ellington; Mills)   F.RCA 741029, Camden
                                                   CDN119, A.RCA CAL459; RCA PM43687

As above.   *New York, May 3, 1929*
51971   COTTON CLUB STOMP (Ellington;   F.RCA 741029, Camden CND
           Mills)   119, A.RCA CAL459
51972   MISTY MORNIN' (Whetsol; Ellington)   F.RCA 741029
51973   ARABIAN LOVER (McHugh; Fields   F.RCA 741029, Camden
                                                   CDN119, A.RCA CAL459

Cootie Williams (tp); Johnny Hodges (a-s); Barney Bigard (cl); Duke Ellington (p);
Fred Guy (bjo); Wellman Braud (b); Sonny Greer (d).   *New York, May 3, 1929*
51974   SARATOGA SWING (Bigard)   F.RCA 741029, Camden
                                                   CDN119, A.RCA CAL459; PM43687

Full band as above, with Juan Tizol (tb) added.   *New York, July 29, 1929*
E30585   BLACK AND BLUE (Waller; Razaf;   Dec AH47, F.MCA 510017; A.
           Brooks)   Dec 79241
E30586   JUNGLE JAMBOREE (Waller; Razaf;   Dec AH47, F.MCA 510017;
           Brooks)   A.Dec 79241

As above.   *August 2, 1929*
402551   JUNGLE JAMBOREE (Waller; Razaf;   WRC SHB58
           Brooks)
402553   SNAKE HIP DANCE (Waller; Razaf; Brooks) WRC SHB58

90

As above.   *New York, September 13, 1929*
E30937   JOLLY WOG (Ellington)   Dec AH23, F.MCA 510017,
                                                               Aus. Swa 50
E30938   JAZZ CONVULSIONS (Ellington)   Dec AH23, F.MCA 510017,
                                                               Aus. Swa 50

As above with Teddy Bunn (g) and unknown French horn in place of Jenkins.
                                             New York, September 16, 1929
55845   MISSISSIPPI DRY (Youmans)   RCA PM43687, F.RCA 741039
55846   THE DUKE STEPS OUT (Ellington;   RCA PM43687, F.RCA 741039
          Hodges; Williams)
55847   HAUNTED NIGHTS (Ellington) RCA PM43687, F.RCA 741039; Camden
                                                  CDN119, A.CAL459
55848   SWANEE SHUFFLE (Berlin)   RCA PM43687, F.RCA 741039

As Six Jolly Jesters: Freddy Jenkins (tp); Joe Nanton (tb); Johnny Hodges (s); Duke
Ellington (p); Fred Guy (bjo); Wellman Braud (b); Sonny Greer (d).
                                                        October 25, 1929
E31301   SIX OR SEVEN TIMES (Waller; Mills)   Dec AH89, A.Dec DL9245,
          (voc. Jenkins & Greer)   FMCA 510101

Freddy Jenkins, Cootie Williams (tp); Joe Nanton (tb); Johnny Hodges (s); Duke
Ellington (p); Teddy Bunn (g) with The Washboard Serenaders. Bruce Randolph
(wbd & voc).   *October 29, 1929*
E31371   GOIN' NUTS (unknown)   Dec AH23, F.MCA 510101
E31372   OKLAHOMA STOMP (Mills)   Dec AH89, Dec DL9245,
                                                        F.MCA 510101

Arthur Whetsol, Freddy Jenkins, Cootie Williams (tp); Joe Nanton, Juan Tizol (tb);
Johnny Hodges, Harry Carney, Barney Bigard (reeds); Duke Ellington (p); Fred
Guy (bjo); Wellman Braud (b); Sonny Greer (d).   *New York, November 20, 1929*
403286   LAZY DUKE (Ellington) (small group)   WRC SHB58
403287   BLUES OF THE VAGABOND   WRC SHB58
          (Ellington)
403288   SYNCOPATED SHUFFLE (Ellington)   WRC SHB58

As above.   *New York, December 10, 1929*
E31508   SWEET MAMA (Ellington)   F.MCA 510101
E31509   WALL STREET WAIL (Ellington;   F.MCA 510101, DecAH23
          Mills)
E31510   CINCINATTI DADDY (Ellington)   F.MCA 510101, Dec AH47

                              1930
As above. Irving Mills (voc).   *New York, March 20, 1930*
E32447   WHEN YOU'RE SMILING (Fisher;   Dec AH89; F.MCA 510031. A.
          Goodwin; Shay)   Dec DL9245, 79241
E32448B   MAORI (Tyers)   Dec AH47; F.MCA 510101; A.
                                                               Dec 79241
E32449   ADMIRATION (Tizol; Mills)   Dec AH47; A. Dec 79241

As above, without Jenkins & with Joe Cornell (accordeon) added.

New York, April 22, 1930

E32612	DOUBLE CHECK STOMP	Dec AH89; A.Dec DL9245,
	(Braud; Hodges; Bigard)	F.MCA 510031
E32613	ACCORDEON JOE	Dec AH89; A.Dec DL9245;
	(Cornell; Wimbrow)	F.MCA 510031
E32614	COTTON CLUB STOMP	Dec AH23; A.Dec DL9245;
	(Ellington; Mills)	F.MCA 510031

As above with Freddy Jenkins (tp);

New York, June 4, 1930

62192	SWEET DREAMS OF LOVE (Ellington; Mills)	RCA PM43697; F.RCA 741039
62193	JUNGLE NIGHTS IN HARLEM (Ellington)	RCA PM43697; F.RCA 741039
62194	SWEET JAZZ O' MINE (Ellington; Mills)	RCA PM43697; F.RCA 741039
62195	SHOUT 'EM, AUNT TILLIE (Ellington; Mills)	RCA PM43697; F.RCA 741039; Camden CND119, A.CAL459

As above, with Charlie Barnet (chimes) added.

New York, August 26, 1930

61011	RING DEM BELLS	RCA PM43697; F.RCA 741048 (Takes 2, 3 & 6);
	(Ellington; Mills)	Camden CND119, A.CAL459
61012	OLD MAN BLUES (Ellington)	RCA PM43697; F.RCA 741048
61013	THREE LITTLE WORDS	F.RCA 741048
	(Kalmar; Ruby)	

As above.

New York, October 14, 1930

404482	BIG HOUSE BLUES (Ellington)	WRC SHB58
404483	ROCKY MOUNTAIN BLUES	WRC SHB58
	(Simmonds)	

As above.

October 17, 1930

E34927	RUNNIN' WILD (Grey; Woods; Gibbs; Harrington)	Dec AH89; F.MCA 510031, A.Dec DL9245

Arthur Whetsol (tp); Joe Nanton (tb); Barney Bigard (cl); Duke Ellington (p); Fred Guy (g); Wellman Braud (b); Sonny Greer (d).

New York, October 17, 1930

E34928	MOOD INDIGO (DREAMY BLUES) (Ellington; Bigard)	Dec AH166; F.MCA 510031

Full band as above. Mills & Benny Payne (voc).

New York, October 27, 1930

E35035	HOME AGAIN BLUES	Dec AH23; F.MCA 510031
	(Berlin; Akst)	
E35036	WANG-WANG BLUES	Dec AH89; A.Dec DL9245;
	(Muella; Johnson; Busse)	F.MCA 510031

As above.		*New York, October 30, 1930*
404519	RING DEM BELLS	CBS 88000; WRC SHB58
	(Ellington; Mills)	
404520	THREE LITTLE WORDS	CBS 88000; WRC SHB58
	(Ruby; Kalmar)	
404521	OLD MAN BLUES (Ellington)	CBS 88000; WRC SHB58
404522	SWEET CHARIOT	CBS 88000; WRC SHB58
	(Ellington; Mills)	
480023	MOOD INDIGO	CBS 88000; WRC SHB58
	(Ellington; Bigard)	
As above as Memphis Hot Shots. Sid Garry (voc).		*New York, November 8, 1930*
404802	I'M SO IN LOVE WITH YOU	WRC SHB58
	(Ellington; Mills)	
404803	I CAN'T REALIZE YOU LOVE ME	WRC SHB58
	(Donaldson; DeSylva)	
404804	ROCKIN' IN RHYTHM	WRC SHB58
	(Ellington; Carney; Mills)	
As above.		*New York, December 10, 1930*
04811	MOOD INDIGO	F.RCA 741068
	(Ellington; Bigard; Mills)	

1931

As above.		*New York, January 14, 1931*
E35800	ROCKIN' CHAIR (Carmichael)	Dec AH166; F.MCA 510101
E35801	ROCKIN' IN RHYTHM	F.MCA 510031
	(Ellington; Carney; Mills)	
E35802	TWELFTH STREET RAG	Dec AH166; F.MCA 510031
	(Bowman)	
As above.		*New York, January 20, 1931*
E35939/40	CREOLE RHAPSODY-Part 1 (Ellington)	Dec AH89; A.Dec DL9245;
		F.MCA 510031
As above.		*Camden, NJ, June 11, 1931*
68231/2	CREOLE RHAPSODY-Parts 1&2 (Ellington)	RCA PM43697;
		F.RCA 741068; Camden CDN119; A.CAL459
As above.		*Camden NJ, June 16, 1931*
68237	LIMEHOUSE BLUES (Braham;	RCA PM43697; F.RCA 741068; A.RCA
	Furber)	LPV506; It. RCA LPM34078
68238	ECHOES OF THE JUNGLE (Ellington)	RCA PM43697,
		F.RCA 741068; A.RCA LPV506; It.RCA LPM34078
As above.		*Camden NJ, June 17, 1931*
68239	IT'S GLORY (Ellington)	RCA PM43697, F.RCA 741085; A.RCA
		LPV506; It.RCA LPM34078
68240	THE MYSTERY SONG (Ellington)	RCA PM43697, F.RCA 741085

Arthur Whetsol, Cootie Williams, Freddy Jenkins (tp); Joe Nanton, Juan Tizol (tb); Barney Bigard, Harry Carney, Johnny Hodges (reeds); Duke Ellington (p); Fred Guy (g); Wellman Braud (b); Sonny Greer (d); Ivie Anderson (voc).

Camden NJ, February 2, 1932

11204	IT DON'T MEAN A THING (Ellington)	RCA PM43697

As above	*Camden NJ, February 9, 1932*	
71838	DINAH (Akst; Lewis; Young)	RCA PM43697; F.RCA 741085 A.RCA LPV506; It.RCA LPM34078
71839	BUGLE CALL RAG (Pettis; Mills; Schoebel)	F.RCA A.RCA LPV506; RCA PM43697; It.RCA LPM34078

As above.		*New York, February 11, 1932*
BX11263	ST. LOUIS BLUES (Handy)	CBS 88035
BX11264	CREOLE LOVE CALL (Ellington; Mills; Jackson)	CBS 88035

As above with Lawrence Brown (tb) & Otto Hardwick (s) added.

New York, May 16, 1932

B11840	THE SHEIK OF ARABY (Snyder)	CBS 88035

As above.		*New York, May 17, 1932*
B11850	SWAMPY RIVER (Ellington)	CBS 88035
B11851	FAST AND FURIOUS (Ellington)	CBS 88035

As above.		*New York, May 18, 1932*
B11865	SLIPPERY HORN (Ellington)	CBS 88035
B11866	BLUE RAMBLE (Ellington)	CBS 88035. 62179, A.Col CL2047

As above.		*New York, September 19, 1932*
B12333	DUCKY WUCKY (Ellington; Bigard)	CBS 62179, A.Col. CL2047

As above.		*New York, September 21, 1932*
B12343	JAZZ COCKTAIL (Carter)	CBS 88035
B12344	LIGHTNIN' (Ellington)	CBS 62179, A.Col CL2047

As above		*New York, September 26, 1932*
73557	MAORI (Tyers)	RCA 741114

As above, with The Mills Brothers (voc)* & Ethel Waters (voc)**. Without Bigard.

New York, December 22, 1932

12781	*DIGA DIGA DOO (McHugh; Fields)	A.Col 6770; CBS 88082
12783	**I CAN'T GIVE YOU ANYTHING BUT LOVE (McHugh; Fields)	A.Col 6770; CBS 88082
12784	**PORGY (McHugh; Fields)	A.Col 6770; CBS 88082

As above, with Barney Bigard. *Ivie Anderson (voc).   *New York, February 15, 1933*
265049   MERRY-GO-ROUND (Ellington)   CBS 88082; WRC SHB42; MFP
                                                                               MFP1085
265050   SOPHISTICATED LADY (Ellington;   CBS 88082; WRC SHB42; MFP
           Mills; Parish)   MFP1085
265051   *I'VE GOT THE WORLD ON A STRING   CBS 88082; WRC SHB42; MFP
           (Arlen; Koehler)   MFP1085

As above.   *February 16, 1933*
265052   DOWN A CAROLINA LANE (Parish;   CBS 88082; WRC SHB42; MFP
           Perkins)   MFP1085

As above.   *February 17, 1933*
B13078   SLIPPERY HORN (Ellington)   CBS 88082, 62179; A.Col. CL2047
B13079/80 BLACKBIRDS MEDLEY (McHugh; Fields)   CBS 88082
B13081   DROP ME OFF AT HARLEM (Ellington)   CBS 88082; 62179; A.Col.
                                                                         CL2047

As above.   *May 16, 1933*
B13337   BUNDLE OF BLUES (Ellington)   CBS 88082, 62179, A.Col. CL2047
B13338   SOPHISTICATED LADY (Ellington; Hardwick; Brown)   CBS 88082
B13339   STORMY WEATHER (Arlen; Koehler)   CBS 88082

As above.   *London, July 13, 1933*
GB6038   HYDE PARK (Ellington)   Dec ACL1176
GB6039   HARLEM SPEAKS (Ellington; Mills)   Dec ACL1176
GB6041   CHICAGO (Fisher)   Dec ACL1176

As above. *Ivie Anderson (voc).   *New York, August 15, 1933*
B13800   *I'M SATISFIED (Ellington; Parish;   CBS 62612, 88087; A.Col. 2364
           Mills)
B13801   JIVE STOMP (Ellington)   CBS 62612, 88087; A.Col. 2364
B13802   HARLEM SPEAKS (Ellington; Mills)   CBS 88137, 62179
B13803   IN THE SHADE OF THE OLD APPLE   CBS 62612, 88137; A.Col.
           TREE (Van Alstyne; Williams)   CL2364

Arthur Whetsol, Cootie Williams, Freddy Jenkins, Louis Bacon (tp); Joe Nanton,
Juan Tizol, Lawrence Brown (tb); Barney Bigard, Johnny Hodges, Otto Hardwick,
Harry Carney (reeds); Duke Ellington (p); Fred Guy (g); Wellman Braud (b);
Sonny Greer (d); *Louis Bacon (voc).   *Chicago, September 26, 1933*
77025   RUDE INTERLUDE (Ellington)   RCA PM43697;
                    A.RCA LPV506; It.RCA LPM34078; A.RCA 741114
77026   DALLAS DOINGS (Ellington)   RCA PM43697;
                    A.RCA LPV506; It.RCA LPM34078; 741114

As above, but without Tizol.   *Chicago, December 4, 1933*
77199   *DEAR OLD SOUTHLAND (Creamer;   RCA PM43697;
           Layton)   A.RCA LPV506; It.RCA LPM34078; Fr. RCA 741114
77201   DAYBREAK EXPRESS (Ellington)   RCA PM43697;
                    A.RCA LPV506; It.RCA LPM34078; Fr. RCA 741114

As above.   *Chicago, January 9, 1934*
80144   DELTA SERENADE (Ellington)   RCA PM43697;
                    A.RCA LPV506; It.RCA LPM34078; Fr. RCA 741114
80145   STOMPY JONES (Ellington)   RCA PM43697;
                    A.RCA LPV506; It.RCA LPM34078; Fr. RCA 741114

As above.   *Chicago, January 10, 1934*
80149   SOLITUDE (Ellington; Mills; DeLange)   RCA PM43697;
                    A.RCA LPV506; LPM34078; Fr. RCA 741114
80150   BLUE FEELING (Ellington)   RCA PM43697;
                    A.RCA LPV506; It.RCA LPM34078; Fr. RCA 741114

As above, but without Bacon & Hardwick.   *Hollywood, April 12, 1934*
79155   EBONY RHAPSODY (Johnston; Coslow)   A.RCA LPV506; It.RCA
                    LPM34078; Fr. RCA FPM1-7002; RCA PM43697
79157   LIVE AND LOVE TONIGHT (Johnston;   A.RCA LPV506; It.RCA
         Coslow)   LPM34078; Fr. RCA FPM1-7002; RCA PM43697

As above, but without Jenkins.   *Hollywood, May 9, 1934*
79211   TROUBLED WATERS (Johnston;   A.RCA LPV506; It.RCA
         Coslow)   LPM34078; Fr. RCA FPM1-7002; RCA PM43697

As above, but with Tizol & Hardwick.   *New York, September 12, 1934*
B15910   SOLITUDE (Ellington)   CBS 88137, 62179; A.Col.
                                                             CL2047
B15911   SADDEST TALE (Ellington; Nanton)   CBS 88137, 62179; A.Col.
                                                             CL2047
B15912   MOON GLOW (Hudson; DeLange;   CBS 88137
         Mills)
B15913   SUMP'N 'BOUT RHYTHM (Ellington)   CBS 88137, 62612; A.Col.
                                                             CL2364

Cootie Williams, Charlie Allen, Rex Stewart (tp); Joe Nanton, Juan Tizol,
Lawrence Brown (tb); Barney Bigard, Otto Hardwick, Johnny Hodges, Harry
Carney (reeds); Duke Ellington (p); Fred Guy (g); Wellman Braud (b); Fred
Avendorf (d).   *New York, April 30, 1935*
B17406   IN A SENTIMENTAL MOOD   CBS 88137, 62612; A.Col.
         (Ellington)   CL2364
B17407   SHOWBOAT SHUFFLE (Ellington)   CBS 88137, 62612; A.Col.
                                                             CL2364
B17408   MERRY-GO-ROUND (Ellington; Mills)   CBS 88137, 62179; A.Col.
                                                             CL2047

As above, but Arthur Whetsol (tp); replaces Allen, Sonny Greer (d) replaces
Avendorf; and Ben Webster (t-s) & Billy Taylor (b) added. Ivie Anderson (voc).
                                                             New York, August 19, 1935
B17974   COTTON (Koehler; Bloom)   CBS 88137
B17975   TRUCKIN' (Koehler; Bloom)   CBS 88137, 62612; A.Col.
                                                             CL2364

As above, without Ben Webster.   *New York, September 12, 1935.*
B18072/3 REMINISCING IN TEMPO (Ellington)   CBS 62612, 88137; A.Col.
                                                              CL2364

                              1936
As above, except that Hayes Alvis (b) replaces Braud & Taylor.
                                                  New York, February 27, 1936.
B18735   (THERE IS) NO GREATER LOVE   CBS 62612, 88140; A. Col
          (Symes; Jones)   CL2364

As above, without Otto Hardwick.   *New York, February 28, 1936.*
B18736   CLARINET LAMENT (BARNEY'S   CBS 62179, 88140; Col. CL2047
          CONCERTO) (Ellington)
B18737   ECHOES OF HARLEM (COOTIE'S   CBS 62179, 88140; A. Col
          CONCERTO) (Ellington)   CL2047

As above with Pete Clark (s) added.   *New York, February 28, 1936.*
B18739   KISSIN' MY BABY GOODNIGHT   CBS 62612, 88140; Col. CL2364
          (David; Meyer; Wendling)

As above, with Hardwick replacing Clark.   *New York, July 17, 1936.*
B19563   IT WAS A SAD NIGHT IN HARLEM   CBS 68223, 88140
          (Lewis; Kresa)
B19564   TRUMPET IN SPADES (Ellington)   CBS 52628, 88140

As above, with Ben Webster (s) added.   *New York, July 29, 1936.*
B19626   IN A JAM (Ellington)   CBS 62179, 88140; A. Col CL2047
B19627   EXPOSITION SWING (Ellington)   CBS 62612, 88140; A. Col CL2364
B19628   UPTOWN DOWNBEAT (Ellington)   CBS 62612, 88140; A. Col CL2364

Rex Stewart (c); Lawrence Brown (tb); Johnny Hodges (a-s, sop-s); Harry Carney
(bar-s); Duke Ellington (p); Ceele Burke (g); Billy Taylor (b); Sonny Greer (d).
                                                  New York, December 16, 1936.
B4369   REXATIOUS (Stewart)   Epic 22006, 24203; CBS 88140,
                                                                        52628
B4370   LAZY MAN'S SHUFFLE (Stewart)   Epic 22006, 24203; CBS 88140,
                                                                        52628

Cootie Williams (tp); Juan Tizol (tb); Barney Bigard, Johnny Hodges, Harry
Carney (reeds); Duke Ellington (p); Billy Taylor (b); Sonny Greer (d).
                                                  New York December 19, 1936.
L0371   CLOUDS IN MY HEART (Bigard;   Epic 22006, 24203; CBS 88140
          Ellington)
L0372   FROLIC SAM (Williams)   Epic 22006; CBS 88140
L0373   CARAVAN (Mills; Ellington; Tizol)   Epic 22006, 24203; CBS 88140
L0374   STOMPY JONES (Ellington)   Epic 22006, 24203; CBS 88140

Wallace Jones, Cootie Williams (tp); Rex Stewart (c); Joe Nanton, Juan Tizol, Lawrence Brown (tb); Barney Bigard, Otto Hardwick, Johnny Hodges, Harry Carney (reeds); Duke Ellington (p); Fred Guy (g); Hayes Alvis, Billy Taylor (b); Sonny Greer (d); Ivie Anderson (voc).   *New York, March 5, 1937*

M177	THE NEW BIRMINGHAM BREAKDOWN (Ellington)	Swe. Tax M-8001; CBS 88140
M178	SCATTIN' AT THE KIT KAT (Ellington; Mills)	Swe. Tax M-8001; CBS 88140
M179	I'VE GOT TO BE A RUG CUTTER (Ellington)	Swe. Tax M-8801; CBS 88185
M180	THE NEW EAST ST. LOUIS TOODLE-OO (Ellington; Miley)	Swe. Tax M-8001; CBS 88185

Cootie Williams (tp); Joe Nanton (tb); Johnny Hodges, Harry Carney (reeds); Duke Ellington (p); Hayes Alvis (b); Sonny Greer (d).   *New York, March 8, 1937*

M185	I CAN'T BELIEVE THAT YOU'RE IN LOVE WITH ME (McHugh; Gaskill)	Epic 22006, 24203; Ph. BBL7163; CBS 88185
M187	DIGA DIGA DOO (McHugh; Fields)	Swe. Tax M-8005; CBS 88185

Cootie Williams, Rex Stewart, Wallace Jones (tp); Joe Nanton, Juan Tizol, Lawrence Brown (tb); Barney Bigard, Johnny Hodges, Otto Hardwick, Harry Carney (reeds); Duke Ellington (p); Fred Guy (g); Billy Taylor, Hayes Alvis (b); Sonny Greer (d).   *New York, May 14, 1937*

M470	CARAVAN (Tizol; Ellington; Mills)	CBS 62179; A. Col CL2047
M471	AZURE (Ellington; Mills)	CBS 62612; A. Col CL2364

As above, Ivie Anderson (voc).   *New York, June 8, 1937*

M519	ALL GOD'S CHILLUN GOT RHYTHM (Kahn; Caper; Jurmann)	CBS 66302; A. Col. CL2365
M521	ALABAMY HOME (Ringle; Ellington)	Swe. Tax M-8001

Rex Stewart (c); Freddie Jenkins (tp); Johnny Hodges, Harry Carney (reeds); Duke Ellington (p); Brick Fleagle (g); Hayes Alvis (b); Jack Maisel (d).   *New York, July 7, 1937*

M549	BACK ROOM ROMP (Stewart; Ellington)	CBS 88210
M550	LOVE IN MY HEART (Alvis; Ellington)	Ep LN24203
M551	SUGAR HILL SHIM SHAM (Stewart; Ellington)	CBS 88210
M552	TEA AND TRUMPETS (Stewart; Ellington)	CBS 88210

As above, without Juan Tizol & Hayes Alvis.   *New York, September 20, 1937*

M646	CHATTER BOX (Stewart; Ellington; Mills)	Swe. Tax M-8001; CBS 88210
M647	JUBILESTA (Ellington; Mills; Tizol)	Swe. Tax M-8021; CBS 88210
M648	DIMINUENDO IN BLUE (Ellington)	CBS 62180, 88210; A. Col CL2048

M649	CRESCENDO IN BLUE (Ellington)	CBS 62180, 88210; A. Col CL2048
M650	HARMONY IN HARLEM (Ellington)	CBS 62179, 88210; A. Col CL2047
M651	DUSK IN THE DESERT (Ellington; Mills)	CBS 66302, 88210; A. Col CL2365

Cootie Williams (tp); Juan Tizol (tb); Barney Bigard, Otto Hardwick, Harry Carney (reeds); Duke Ellington (p); Billy Taylor (b); Sonny Greer (d).

New York, October 26, 1937

| M670 | WATCHIN' (Mills; Nemo) | CBS 88220; Swe. Tax M-8005 |
| M671 | PIGEONS AND PEPPERS (D. & M. Ellington) | CBS 88220; Swe. Tax M-8005 |

1938

As previous full band with Baker (tp); & Alvis (b).   *New York, January 13, 1938*

| M713 | STEPPIN' INTO SWING SOCIETY (Ellington; Nemo; Mills) | CBS 66302, 88220; A. Col CL2365 |

Cootie Williams (tp); Lawrence Brown (tb); Johnny Hodges, Harry Carney, Barney Bigard or Otto Hardwick (reeds); Duke Ellington (p); Fred Guy (g); Billy Taylor (b); Sonny Greer (d).   *New York, January 19, 1938*

M726	HAVE A HEART (Tizol, Ellington; Singer; Mills)	Epic 24250; Ph. BBL7163; CBS 88220
M727	MY DAY	Swe. Tax M-8022; CBS 88220
M728	SILV'RY MOON	Swe. Tax M-8022; CBS 88220
M729	ECHOES OF HARLEM (Ellington)	Epic 24203, 22006; CBS 88220

Full band as above.   *New York, February 2, 1938*

| M751 | RIDING ON A BLUE NOTE (Ellington; Mills) | CBS 62180, 88220; A. Col CL2048 |
| M753 | THE GAL FROM JOE'S (Ellington; Mills) | CBS 62180, 88220; A. Col CL2048 |

As above.   *New York, March 3, 1938*

| M772 | I LET A SONG GO OUT OF MY HEART (Ellington; Nemo; Mills) | CBS 62180, 88220; A. Col. CL2048 |
| M773 | BRAGGIN' IN BRASS (Ellington; Nemo; Mills) | Swe. Tax M-8000; CBS 88220 |

Cootie Williams (tp); Lawrence Brown (tb); Johnny Hodges (alt); Harry Carney (bar); Duke Ellington (p); Billy Taylor (b); Sonny Greer (d).

New York, March 28, 1938

M793	JEEP'S BLUES (Ellington; Hodges)	CBS 52587, 88220
M794	IF YOU WERE IN MY PLACE (Ellington; Nemo; Mills)	Swe. Tax M-8022; CBS 88220
M795	I LET A SONG GO OUT OF MY HEART (Ellington; Nemo; Mills)	Swe. Tax M-8022; CBS 88220
M796	RENDEZVOUS WITH RHYTHM (Ellington; Hodges)	CBS 52587

Cootie Williams (tp); Joe Nanton (tb); Johnny Hodges, Otto Hardwick, Barney Bigard, Harry Carney (reeds); Duke Ellington (p); Fred Guy (g); Billy Taylor (b); Sonny Greer (d); Jerry Kruger (voc).   *New York, April 4, 1938*

| M802 | SWINGTIME IN HONOLULU (Ellington) | Swe. Tax M-8005;CBS 88242 |
| M803 | CARNIVAL IN CAROLINE (Ellington; Nemo; Mills) | Swe. Tax M-8005; CBS 88242 |

Cootie Williams, Rex Stewart, Harold Baker, Wallace Jones (tp); Joe Nanton, Juan Tizol, Lawrence Brown (tb); Barney Bigard, Johnny Hodges, Otto Hardwick, Harry Carney (reeds); Duke Ellington (p); Fred Guy (g); Billy Taylor (b); Sonny Greer (d). [Full band personnel]   *New York, April 11, 1938*

As above, without Harold Baker.   *New York, June 7, 1938*
| M834 | PYRAMID(Ellington; Gordon; Tizol) | CBS 66302, 88242; A. Col CL2365 |

As above.   *New York, June 20, 1938*
| M845 | A GYPSY WITHOUT A SONG (Ellington; Tizol; Gordon; Singer) | CBS 66302, 88242; A. Col CL2365 |

Cootie Williams (tp); Lawrence Brown (tb); Johnny Hodges, Harry Carney (reeds); Duke Ellington (p); Billy Taylor (b); Sonny Greer (d).   *New York, June 22, 1938*
| M852 | YOU WALKED OUT OF THE PICTURE (Little: Oppenheim; Tobias) | Swe. Tax M-8022; CBS 88242 |
| M853 | PYRAMID (Ellington; Tizol; Gordon) | Epic 24203, 22006; Ph BBL7163 |

As above.   *New York, July 1, 1938*
| M875 | JITTERBUG'S LULLABY (Ellington; Hodges; Mills) | Epic 22006, 24203; Ph CBS 88243, BBL7163 |

Cootie Williams (tp); Barney Bigard, Johnny Hodges, Otto Hardwick, Harry Carney (reeds); Duke Ellington (p); Billy Taylor (b); Sonny Greer (d).
                              New York, August 3, 1938
| M878 | SHARPIE (Mills) | Swe. Tax M-8005 |
| M879 | SWING PAN ALLEY (Ellington; Williams) | Epic 24203, 22006; Ph. BBL7163 |

Full band as previous above.   *New York, August 9, 1938*
| M884 | PRELUDE TO A KISS (Ellington; Gordon; Mills) | CBS 62180; A. Col CL2048 |
| M886 | BUFFET FLAT (Ellington) | CBS 66302; A. Col CL2365 |

Cootie Williams (tp); Lawrence Brown (tb); Johnny Hodges, Harry Carney (reeds); Duke Ellington (p); Billy Taylor (b); Sonny Greer (d); Mary HcHugh (voc).
                              New York, August 24, 1938
M887	PRELUDE TO A KISS (Ellington; Gordon; Mills)	Epic 24250
M888	THERE'S SOMETHING ABOUT AN OLD LOVE (Hudson)	Swe. Tax M-8022
M889	THE JEEP IS JUMPIN' (Ellington; Hodges)	Epic 24250
M890	KRUM ELBOW BLUES (Ellington; Hodges)	CBS 52587

Full band, as above.   *New York, December 19, 1938*
M947   JAZZ POTPOURRI (MYRTLE AVENUE   CBS 62180; A. Col CL2048
          STOMP) (Ellington)
M949   BATTLE OF SWING (Ellington)   CBS 62180; A. Col CL2048

Cootie Williams (tp); Harry Carney (bar); Johnny Hodges (alt); Barney Bigard (clt); Duke Ellington (p); Billy Taylor (b); Sonny Greer (d).
                                           New York, December 21, 1938
M954   DELTA MOOD (Ellington)   Epic 24250
M955   THE BOYS FROM HARLEM (Ellington)   Swe. Tax M-8005
M956   MOBILE BLUES (Ellington)   Epic 24250; Ph. BBL7163
M957   GAL-A-VANTIN' (Ellington)   Swe. Tax M-8005

Full band, as above.   *New York, December 22, 1938*
M958   BLUE LIGHT (Ellington)
M959   OLD KING DOOJI (Ellington)   CBS 66302; A. Col CL2365
M960   BOY MEETS HORN (Ellington; Stewart)   CBS 62180; A. Col CL2048
M961   SLAP HAPPY (Ellington)   CBS 62180; A. Col CL2048

1939

Cootie Williams (tp); Lawrence Brown (tb); Johnny Hodges, Harry Carney (reeds); Duke Ellington (p); Billy Taylor (b); Sonny Greer (d).   *New York, February 27, 1939*
M976   SWINGIN' ON THE CAMPUS   Epic 24250; Ph. BBL7163
          (Ellington; Hodges)
M977   DOOJI WOOJI (Ellington)   CBS 52587

Cootie Williams (tp); Harry Carney, Johnny Hodges, Otto Hardwick, Barney Bigard (reeds); Duke Ellington (p); Billy Taylor (b); Sonny Greer (d).
                                        New York, February 28, 1939
M982   BEAUTIFUL ROMANCE (Ellington)   Swe. Tax M-8005
M983   BOUDOIR BENNY (Ellington; Williams)   Swe. Tax M-8005
M985   SHE'S GONE (Ellington)   Swe. Tax M-8005

Rex Stewart (c); Louis Bacon (tp); Joe Nanton (tb); Barney Bigard (clt); Duke Ellington (p); Billy Taylor (b); Sonny Greer (d).   *New York, March 20, 1939*
M994   SAN JUAN HILL (Ellington; Stewart;   Epic 24250; Ph. BBL7163; CBS
          Fleagle)   52628
M995   I'LL COME BACK FOR MORE   Epic 24250; CBS 52628
          (Ellington; Stewart; Fleagle)
M996   FAT STUFF SERENADE (Ellington;   Epic 24250; Ph. BBL7163; CBS
          Stewart)   52628

Wallace Jones, Cootie Williams (tp); Rex Stewart (c); Joe Nanton, Juan Tizol, Lawrence Brown (tb); Johnny Hodges, Otto Hardwick, Barney Bigard, Harry Carney (reeds); Duke Ellington (p); Billy Taylor (b); Fred Guy (g); Sonny Greer (d).   *New York, March 20, 1939*
M997   PUSSY WILLOW (Ellington)   CBS 66302; A. Col CL2365
M998   SUBTLE LAMENT (Ellington)   CBS 62180; A. Col CL2048
M1000   SMORGASBORD AND SCHNAPPS (Ellington)   Swe. Tax 8010

Johnny Hodges (alt); Duke Ellington (p); Billy Taylor (b).   *New York, March 21, 1939*
WM1005   FINESSE (Ellington)   Epic 22002

Full band as above, Billy Strayhorn (p) on *.   *New York, March 21, 1939*
WM1006   PORTRAIT OF THE LION (Ellington)   CBS 62180, A. Col CL2048
WM1007   *SOMETHING TO LIVE FOR   CBS 66302, A. Col CL2365
         (Ellington; Strayhorn)

Full band, as above.   *New York, June 6, 1939*
WM1032   WAY LOW (Ellington)   CBS 66302; A. Col CL2365
WM1033   SERENADE TO SWEDEN (Ellington)   CBS 66302; A. Col CL2365

Full band, as above, Ivie Anderson (voc).   *June 12, 1939*
WM1039   I'M CHECKIN' OUT, GOO'M BYE   CBS 66302; A. Col CL 2365
         (Bigard; Ellington)

Cootie Williams (tp); Johnny Hodges (alt); Otto Hardwick (alt); Harry Carney (bar);
Duke Ellington (p); Billy Taylor (b); Sonny Greer (d).   *New York, June 22, 1939*
WM1042   NIGHT SONG (Tizol; Mundy)   Swe. Tax M-8005
WM1045   BLACK BEAUTY (Ellington)   Swe. Tax M-8005

Full band, as above.   *New York, August 28, 1939*
WM1063   THE SERGEANT WAS SHY (Ellington)   CBS 62280; A. Col CL2048

Cootie Williams (tp); Lawrence Brown (tb); Johnny Hodges, Harry Carney (reeds);
Billy Strayhorn (p); Billy Taylor (b); Sonny Greer (d).   *New York, September 1, 1939*
WM1072   THE RABBIT'S JUMP (Hodges)   Epic 220066, 24203; Ph. BBL7163
WM1075   DREAM BLUES (Hodges)   CBS 52587

Full band, as above, but Jimmy Blanton (b) replaces Taylor.
                                                            New York, October 14, 1939
WM1091   LITTLE POSEY (Ellington)   CBS 66302; A. Col CL2365
WM1093   GRIEVIN' (Strayhorn; Ellington)   CBS 62180; A. Col CL2048
WM1094   TOOTIN' THROUGH THE ROOF   CBS 66302, 62613; A. Col
         (Ellington)   CL2365
WM1095   WEELY (Ellington)   CBS 66302; A. Col CL2365

Rex Stewart (c); Juan Tizol (tp); Barney Bigard (cl); Harry Carney (bar); Duke
Ellington (p); Jimmy Blanton (b); Sonny Greer (d).   *New York, November 22, 1939*
WM1117   MINUET IN BLUES (Ellington)   Swe. Tax M-8023
WM1118   LOST IN TWO FLATS (Strayhorn)   Swe. Tax M-8023
WM1119   HONEY HUSH (Bigard; Ellington)   Swe. Tax M-8023

Wallace Jones, Cootie Williams (tp); Rex Stewart (c); Joe Nanton, Juan Tizol, Lawrence Brown (tb); Barney Bigard, Otto Hardwick, Johnny Hodges, Harry Carney, Ben Webster (reeds); Duke Ellington (p); Fred Guy (g); Jimmy Blanton (b); Sonny Greer (d); Ivie Anderson (voc). *New York, 14 February, 1940*

WM1135	SOLITUDE (Ellington; Mills; DeLange)	CBS 68223
WM1136	STORMY WEATHER (Arlen; Koehler)	CBS 68223, 62180; A. Col CL2048
WM1137	MOOD INDIGO (Ellington; Bigard; Mills)	CBS 68223
WM1138	SOPHISTICATED LADY (Ellington; Mills; Parish)	CBS 68223, 62180; A. Col CL2048

Rex Stewart (c); Juan Tizol (tb); Barney Bigard (cl); Harry Carney (bar); Duke Ellington (p); Jimmy Blanton (b); Sonny Greer (d). *New York, February 14, 1940*

WM1139	PELICAN DRAG (Carney)	Ph. BBL7163
WM1140	TAPIOLA (Strayhorn)	Swe. Tax M-8023
WM1141	MARDI GRAS MADNESS (Bigard; Ellington)	Swe. Tax M-8023
WM1142	WATCH THE BIRDIE (Raye; De Paul)	Swe. Tax M-8023

Full orchestra, as above. Herb Jeffries (voc) added. *Chicago, March 6, 1940*

044887	YOU, YOU DARLIN' (Scholl; Jerome)	F.RCA FPM1-7002
044888	JACK THE BEAR (Ellington)	RCA 730565, A. LPM-1715, LSA-3071; RD-27133, 7002; A. Sm RO13; R.RCA FMI-7002; PM45352
044889	KO-KO (Ellington)	RCA 730565, A.LPM-1715, RD-27133, 7002; A. Sm. RO13; F.RCA FPM1-7002; RCA PM45352
044890	MORNING GLORY (Ellington; Stewart)	RCA 730559, 7002, RD-27258; A. Sm. RO13; A. LPM6009/1; PM45352; F.RCA FPMI-7002
044891	SO FAR, SO GOOD (Lawrence; Mundy; White)	F.RCA FPM1-7002

As above. *Chicago, March 15, 1940*

049015	CONGA BRAVA (Ellington; Tizol)	RCA 7047, A. Sm. RO13; RCA PM45352; F.RCA FPM1-7047
049016	CONCERTO FOR COOTIE (Ellington; Russell)	RCA 730565, A. LPM-1715, ISA-3071; RD-27133, 7047; A. Sm. RO13; F.RCA FPM7-7047; PM45352
049017	ME AND YOU (Ellington)	A. Sm. RO13 F.RCA FPM1-7047

As above. *Hollywood, May 4, 1940*

049655	COTTON TAIL (Ellington)	RCA RD-27134, LSA-3069; 730567, 7047; PM45352; A. LPM-1364; A.Sm. RO13; F.RCA FPM1-7047
049656	NEVER NO LAMENT (DON'T GET AROUND MUCH ANYMORE) (Ellington)	RCA, 730567; PM45352; A. Sm. RO13; F.RCA FPM1-7047

As above.   *Chicago, May 28, 1940*

053020   DUSK (Ellington)   RCA 750559, PM45352;
                                                A. SM. RO13; F.RCA FPM1-7047

053021   BOJANGLES (Ellington)   F.RCA FPM1-7047, RD-27258;
                                     A. Sm. RO13; A.RCA LPM6009/1;
                                             PM45352

053022   PORTRAIT OF BERT WILLIAMS   RCA 730567; F.RCA-
        (Ellington)   FPM1-7047, RD-27134;
                                     LSA-3069 A. Sm. RO13' A.
                                  RCA LPM-1364, PM45352

053023   BLUE GOOSE (Ellington)   F.RCA FPM1-7047; Sm RO13

As above. *Ivie Anderson (voc).   *New York, July 22, 1940*

054606   HARLEM AIR-SHAFT (Ellington)   RCA 730565, F.RCA
                                     FPM1-7047, LPM-1715,
                     RD-27133; PM45352; A. Sm. RO13

054607   *AT A DIXIE ROADSIDE DINER (Burke;   A. Sm. RO13; F.RCA
        Leslie)   FPM1-1047; PM45352

054608   ALL TOO SOON (Ellington; Sigman)   RCA 730567, RD-27134,
                                   LSA-3069; A. Sm. RO13; A.RCA
                    LPM-1364; F.RCA FPM1-1047; PM45352

054609   RUMPUS IN RICHMOND (Ellington)   RCA 730567, F.RCA
                                     FPM1-7047, RD-27134,
                                   LSA-3069; A. Sm. RO13;
                                  A.RCA LPM-1364; PM45352

As above.   *New York, July 24, 1940*

054624   MY GREATEST MISTAKE (Fulton; O'Brien)   Fr. RCA FXM17072

054625   SEPIA PANORAMA (Ellington)   RCA 730567, RD-27134, LSA-
                                     3069; A. Sm. RO13; Fr. RCA
                                   FXM17072 (2); A. RCA LPM-
                                   1364; PM45352

As above.   *Chicago, September 5, 1940*

053427   THERE SHALL BE NO NIGHT (Shelley;   Fr. RCA FXM17072;PM45352
        Silver)

053428   IN A MELLOTONE (Ellington)   RCA 730567, RD-27134;
                    A. Sm. RO13; Fr. RCA FXM17072; PM45352

053429   FIVE O'CLOCK WHISTLE (Gannon;   RCA PM45352;
        Myrow; Irwin)   Fr.RCA FXM17072

053430   WARM VALLEY (Ellington)   RCA 730567, RD-27133,
                        A.LPM-1715, A. Sm. RO13; PM45352
                Fr.RCA FXM17072; F.RCA FXM 17094 (Takes 1&2)

Duke Ellington (p); Jimmy Blanton (b).   *Chicago, October 1, 1940*

053504   PITTER PANTHER PATTER (Ellington)   RCA 75489, RD-27258; A. Sm.
                                     RO13; Fr.RCA FXM17072;
                                     A.LPM-6009/1; PM45352

053505   BODY AND SOUL (Heyman; Sour;   RCA 75489, A. Sm. RO13;
        Eyton; Green)   PM45352; F.RCA FXM17072

| 053506 | SOPHISTICATED LADY (Ellington; Mills; Parish) | RCA 75489; A. Sm. RO13; PM45352; F.RCA 1-7072 |
| 053507 | MR. J. B. BLUES (Ellington; Blanton) | RCA 75489, RD-27258; A. Sm. RO13; PM45352; F.RCA 1-7072 |

Full band, as above   *New York, October 17, 1940*

| 053552 | THE FLAMING SWORD (Ellington) | RCA 730567, RD-27134, LSA-30691; F.RCA 17094 |

As above.   *Chicago, October 28, 1940*

053579	ACROSS THE TRACK BLUES (Ellington)	F.RCA FXM 1-7094; A. Sm. RO13; PM45352
053580	CHLOE-E (Kahn; Moret)	RCA RD27133, A. LPM-1715; PM45352; F.RCA FXM 1-7094
053581	I NEVER FELT THIS WAY BEFORE (Ellington)	F.RCA FXM 1-7094; A. Sm. RO13

Cootie Williams (tp); Lawrence Brown (tb); Johnny Hodges (alt, sop); Harry Carney (bar); Duke Ellington (p); Jimmy Blanton (b); Sonny Greer (d).

Chicago, November 2, 1940

053603	DAY DREAM (Strayhorn; Ellington)	RCA 430629, A. LPV-533, Ger. LPM-533; F.RCA FXM 1-7094; NL89582
053604	GOOD QUEEN BESS (Hodges; Mills)	RCA 430629, A. LPV-533, Ger. LPM-533; F.RCA FXM 1-7094; NL89582
053605	THAT'S THE BLUES, OLD MAN (Hodges; Mills)	RCA 430629, A. LPV-533, Ger. LPM-533; F.RCA FXM 1-7094; NL89582
053606	JUNIOR HOP (Ellington)	RCA 430629, A. LPV-533. Ger. LPM-533; F.RCA FXM 1-7094; NL89582

Rex Stewart (c); Lawrence Brown (tb); Ben Webster (ten); Harry Carney (bar); Duke Ellington (p); Jimmy Blanton (b); Sonny Greer (d). *Chicago, November 2, 1940*

053607	WITHOUT A SONG (Rose; Eliscu; Youmans)	RCA LPV-533, Ger. LPM-533; F.RCA FXM 1-7133; NL89582
053608	MY SUNDAY GAL (Ellington)	RCA LPV-533, Ger. LPM-533; F.RCA FXM 1-7133; NL89582
053609	MOBILE BAY (Stewart; Ellington)	RCA LPV-533, Ger. LPM-533; F.RCA FXM 1-7133; NL89582
053610	LINGER AWHILE (Owens; Rose) (Strayhorn (p) on this title)	RCA LPV-533, Ger. LPM-533; F.RCA FXM 1-7133; NL89582

Full band, as above, except that Ray Nance (tp) replaces Williams.

Chicago, December 28, 1940

| 053780 | SIDEWALKS OF NEW YORK (Lawlor; Blake) | F.RCA FXM 1-7134; A. Sm. RO13; PM45352 |

1941

Full band, as above except Billy Strayhorn (p) replaces Ellington.

Hollywood, February 15, 1941

055283	TAKE THE 'A' TRAIN (Strayhorn)	RCA 730567, RD-27134, LSA-3069 FXM 1-7134 A.LPM-1364; NL89274
055284	JUMPIN' PUNKINS (M. Ellington)	F.RCA FXM 1-7134; NL89274
055285	JOHN HARDY'S WIFE(M. Ellington)	F.RCA FXM 1-7134; NL89274
055286	BLUE SERGE (M. Ellington)	RCA 730567, RD-27134, LSA-3069 FXM 1-7134; A. LPM-1364; NL89274

Duke Ellington (p).

New York May 14, 1941

| 065504 | DEAR OLD SOUTHLAND (Creamer; Layton) | RCA 430689, F.RCA FXM 1-7134; NL89582 |
| 065505 | SOLITUDE (Ellington; Mills; De Lange) | RCA 430689, F.RCA FXM 1-7134; NL89582 |

Ray Nance, Rex Stewart, Wallace Jones (tp); Lawrence Brown, Juan Tizol, Joe Nanton (tb); Barney Bigard, Johnny Hodges, Otto Hardwick, Ben Webster, Harry Carney (reeds); Duke Ellington (p); Fred Guy (g); Jimmy Blanton (b); Sonny Greer (d).

Hollywood, June 5, 1941

061283	BAKIFF (Tizol)	F.RCA FXM 1-7135; NL89274
061284	ARE YOU STICKIN' (Ellington)	F.RCA FXM 1-7135; NL89274
061285	JUST A-SETTIN' AND A-ROCKIN' (Ellington; Strayhorn; Gaines)	RCA 730567, RD-27134, LSA-3069; A. LPM-1364 F.RCA FXM 1-7135; NL89274
061286	THE GIDDYBUG GALLOP (Ellington)	F.RCA FXM 1-7135; NL89274

As above. Ivie Anderson (voc).

Hollywood, June 26, 1941

| 061318 | CHOCOLATE SHAKE (Ellington; Webster) | F.RCA FXM 1-7135; NL89274 |
| 061319 | I GOT IT BAD AND THAT AIN'T GOOD (Ellington; Webster) | F.RCA FXM 1-7135; RCA 730567, RD-27134, LSA-3069; A. PLM-1364; NL89274 |

Rex Stewart (c); Lawrence Brown (tb); Johnny Hodges, Harry Carney (reeds); Duke Ellington (p); Jimmy Blanton (b); Sonny Greer (d).   *Hollywood, July 3, 1941*

061342	SOME SATURDAY (Stewart)	RCA LPV-533, Ger. RCA LPM-533, F.RCA FXM 1-7201; NL89582
061343	SUBTLE SLOUGH (Ellington)	RCA LPV-533, Ger. RCA LPM-533, F.RCA FXM 1-7201; NL89582
061344	MENELIK (THE LION OF JUDAH) (Stewart)	A. RCA LPV-533; Ger. RCA LPM-533, F.RCA FXM 1-7201; NL89582
061345	POOR BUBBER (Stewart)	A. RCA LPV-533; Ger. RCA LPM-533, F.RCA FXM 1-7201; NL89582

Ray Nance (tp); Lawrence Brown (tb); Johnny Hodges, Harry Carney (reeds);
Duke Ellington (p); Jimmy Blanton (b); Sonny Greer (d).   *Hollywood, July 3, 1941*
061346   SQUATY ROO (Hodges)   RCA 430629, A. RCA LPV-533, Ger. RCA
                                     LPM-533, F.RCA FXM 1-7201; NL89582
061347   PASSION FLOWER (Strayhorn RCA 430629, A. RCA LPV-533, Ger. RCA
                                     LPM-533, F.RCA FXM 1-7201; NL89582
061348   THINGS AIN'T WHAT THEY USED TO   RCA 430629, A. RCA LPV-533,
          BE (M. Ellington; Persons)   Ger. RCA LPM-533, F.RCA FXM 1-7201;
                                                                      NL89582
061349   GOIN' OUT THE BACK WAY (Hodges)   RCA 430629, A. RCA LPV-533,
                                     Ger. RCA LPM-533, F.RCA FXM 1-7201; NL89582

Full band, as above, except that Jimmy Bryant (b) replaces Blanton.
                                          Hollywood, September 26, 1941
061684   FIVE O'CLOCK DRAG   RCA 730559, F.RCA FXM 1-7201
          (Ellington)   NL89274
061685   ROCKS IN MY BED   RCA 730567, RD-27134, LSA-3069;
          (Ellington)   A. LPM-1364 F.RCA FXM 1-7201; NL89274

As above, except that Junior Raglin replaces Bryant. Herb Jeffries (voc).
                                          Hollywood, December 2, 1941
061943   I DON'T KNOW WHAT KIND OF BLUES   RCA RD27134, 730567,
          I GOT (Ellington)   LSA-3069; A. LPM-1364
                                          F.RCA FXM 1-7274; NL89274
061687   CHELSEA BRIDGE (Strayhorn)   RCA RD-27258, 730559;
                                     A. LPM 6009/1 F.RCA FXM; 1-7274; NL89274

                                 1942
Full band as above.   *Chicago, January 21, 1942*
070682   PERDIDO (Tizol)   RCA 730567, RD-27134, LSA-3069;
                                     A. LPM-1364 F.RCA FXM 1-7274; NL89274
070683   THE "C" JAM BLUES (Ellington)   RCA 730559, RD-7888,
                                     A. LPV-541 F.RCA FXM1-7274; NL89274
070684   MOON MIST (M. Ellington)   RCA 730559, RD-7888,
                                     LPV-541 F.RCA FXM1-7301; NL89274

As above.   *New York, February 26, 1942*
071890   WHAT AM I HERE FOR? (Ellington)   RCA 730567, RD-27134,
          LSA-3069; A. LPM-1364, F.RCA FXM1-7301; NL89274
071891   I DON'T MIND (Strayhorn; Ellington)   RCA RD-7888, A. LPV-541,
                                          F.RCA FXM1-7301; NL89274
071892   SOMEONE (Ellington)   RCA RD-7888, A. LPV-541,
                                          RCA FXM1-7301; NL89274

As above.   *Hollywood, June 26, 1942*
072438   MAINSTEM (Ellington)   RCA 730567, RD-27134, LSA-3069;
                                     A. LPM-1364, F.RCA FXM1-7301; NL89274
072439   JOHNNY COME LATELY   RCA RD-7888, A. LPV-541,
          (Strayhorn)   F.RCA FXM1-7301; NL89274

As above, except that Chauncey Haughton replaces Bigard. Ivie Anderson (voc).

Chicago, July 28, 1942

074781	HAYFOOT, STRAWFOOT (Lenk; Drake; McGrane)	RCA RD-7888, A. LPV-541, F.RCA FXM1-7301; NL89274
074782	SENTIMENTAL LADY (Ellington)	F.RCA FXM1-7301; NL89274
074783	A SLIP OF THE LIP (Henderson; Mercer)	RCA RD-7888, A. LPV-541, F.RCA FXM1-7301; NL89274
074784	SHERMAN SHUFFLE (Ellington)	RCA RD-7888, A. LPV-541, F.RCA FXM1-7301; NL89274

The 1943/4 recording gap was filled by issues of various Carnegie Hall Concert recordings: January 1943 (A. Prestige P. 34004 [3]); December 1944 (P. 24073 [2]); also January 1946 (P. 24074 [2]) and December 1947 (P. 24075 [2]).

1944

Shelton Hemphill, Ray Nance, Taft Jordan, Cat Anderson (tp); Lawrence Brown, Claude Jones, Joe Nanton (tb); Jimmy Hamilton, Johnny Hodges, Otto Hardwick, Al Sears, Harry Carney (reeds); Duke Ellington (p); Fred Guy (g); Alvin Raglin (b); Sonny Greer (d); Al Hibbler, Kay Davis (voc).   *New York, December 1, 1944*

D4-VB-453	I AIN'T GOT NOTHIN' BUT THE BLUES (Ellington; George)	RCA RD-7888, A. LPV-541, F. FXM1-7302
D4-VB-454	I'M BEGINNING TO SEE THE LIGHT (Ellington; James; George)	F.RCA FXM1-7302
D4-VB-455	DON'T YOU KNOW I CARE (Ellington; David)	F.RCA FXM1-7302
D4-VB-456	I DIDN'T KNOW ABOUT YOU (Ellington; Russell)	F.RCA FXM1-7302, RD-27258

As above, with Joya Sherrill (voc) added.   *New York, December 11, 1944*
BLACK, BROWN AND BEIGE SUITE:

D4-VC-560	WORK SONG (Ellington)	RCA RD-27133, A. LPM-1715; F. FXM1-7302
D4-VC-561	COME SUNDAY (Ellington)	RCA RD-27133, A. LPM-1715

As above.   *New York, December 12, 1944*

D4-VC-562	THE BLUES (Ellington)	RCA RD-27133, A. LPM-1715
D4-VC-563	THREE DANCES (Ellington)	RCA-27133, A. LPM-1715

1945

As above, with Rex Stewart (c) added   *New York, January 4, 1945*

D5-VB-12	CARNEGIE BLUES (Ellington)	F.RCA FXM-7302
D5-VB-13	BLUE CELLOPHANE (Ellington)	F.RCA FXM-7302
D5-VB-14	THE MOOD TO BE WOOED (Hodges; Ellington)	RCA RD-7888, A. LPV-541, F. FXM1-7302
D5-VB-15	MY HEART SINGS (Ellington)	F.RCA FXM-7302

As above, with Rex Stewart (c) added. Ray Nance (voc).　　*New York, May 1, 1945*
D5-VB-232　KISSING BUG (Ellington)　　　　　　　　　　　　RCA FXM1-7303
D5-VB-233　EV'RYTHING BUT YOU (Ellington;　RCA RD-7888, A. LPV-541, F.
　　　　　　Jamis; George)　　　　　　　　　　　　　　　　　FXM1-7303
D5-VB-234　RIFF STACCATO (Schwartz;　　　　RCA RD-7888, A. LPV-541, F.
　　　　　　Orent)　　　　　　　　　　　　　　　　　　　　 FXM1-7303

As above.　　　　　　　　　　　　　　　　　　　　　　*New York, May 10, 1945*
D5-VB-261　PRELUDE TO A KISS (Ellington;　　RCA RD-7888, A. LPV-541, F.
　　　　　　Gordon; Mills)　　　　　　　　　　　　　　　　 FXM1-7303
D5-VB-262　CARAVAN (Ellington; Tizol)　　　　RCA RD-7888, A. LPV-541, F.
　　　　　　　　　　　　　　　　　　　　　　　　　　　　　 FXM1-7303
D5-VB-263　BLACK AND TAN FANTASY　　　　　　　　　　　 RCA FXM1-7303
　　　　　　(Miley; Ellington)
D5-VB-264　MOOD INDIGO (Ellington; Bigard)　　　　　　　　RCA FXM1-7303

As above, except that Bob Haggart (b) replaces Raglin. Joya Sherrill, Marie
Ellington & Kay Davis (voc).　　　　　　　　　　　　　*New York, May 14, 1945*
D5-VB-265　IN A SENTIMENTAL MOOD　　　　　　　　　　F.RCA FXM1-7303
　　　　　　(Ellington; Mills)
D5-VB-266　IT DON'T MEAN A THING IF IT　　　　RCA RD-7888, A. LPV-541,
　　　　　　AIN'T GOT THAT SWING (Ellington)　　　　　　F. FXM1-7303

As above.
D5-AB-268　TONIGHT I SHALL SLEEP　　　　　　　　　　 F.RCA FXM1-7303

As above. Al Hibbler (voc).　　　　　　　　　　　　　*New York, July 24, 1945*
D5-0506/7/16/19　PERFUME SUITE (Ellington)　　RCA RD-27259, F. PM42047

1946
Shelton Hemphill, Ray Nance, Harold Baker, Taft Jordan, Cat Anderson, Francis
Williams (tp); Lawrence Brown, Claude Jones, Wilbur de Paris, Joe Nanton (tb);
Jimmy Hamilton, Johnny Hodges, Russell Procope, Al Sears, Harry Carney (reeds);
Duke Ellington (p); Fred Guy (g); Oscar Pettiford (b); Sonny Greer (d); Kay Davis
(voc); Al Hibbler (voc).　　　　　　　　　　　　　　　*Hollywood, July 9, 1946*
D6-VB-2905　TRANSBLUCENCY (Ellington;　　　RCA RD-27133, A. LPM-1715,
　　　　　　Brown)　　　　　　　　　　　　　　　　　F. PM42397

As above, without Joe Nanton.　　　　　　　　*Hollywood, September 3, 1946*
D6-VB-2131　ROYAL GARDEN BLUES (C.　　　　RCA RD-27133, A. LPM-1715,
　　　　　　Williams; S. Williams)　　　　　　　　　　F.RCA PM42415

As above, without Cat Anderson (tp).　　　　　　*New York, October 23, 1946*
5765　DIMINUENDO IN BLUE (Ellington)　　　Em 3327; Festival 130; Prestige
　　　　　　　　　　　　　　　　　　　　　　　　　　　　　PR24029
5766　MAGENTA HAZE (Ellington)　Em 3327: Festival 130; Prestige PR24029

As above with Cat Anderson.		*New York, November 25, 1946*
5813	SULTRY SUNSET (Ellington)	Em 5327; Festival 130; Prestige PR24029
5814	HAPPY-GO-LUCKY LOCAL, Pt. 2 (Ellington)	Em 5327; Festival 130; Prestige PR24209
5815	TRUMPET NO END (BLUE SKIES) (Berlin)	Em 5327; Festival 130; Prestige PR 24029
5816	HAPPY-GO-LUCKY LOCAL, Pt. 1 (Ellington)	Em 5327; Festival 130; Prestige PR24029
5817	BEAUTIFUL INDIANS (HIAWATHA) (Ellington)	Em 5327; Festival 130; Prestige PR24029
5818	FLIPPANT FLURRY (Ellington)	Em 5327; Festival 130; Prestige PR24029

As above without Anderson.		*New York, December 5, 1946*
5823	GOLDEN FEATHER (Ellington)	Em 5327; Festival 130; Prestige PR24029
5824	BEAUTIFUL INDIANS (MINNEHAHA) (Ellington)	Em 5327; Festival 130; Prestige PR 24029

As above.		*New York, December 18, 1946*
5845/6	OVERTURE TO A JAM SESSION (Strayhorn)	Em 5327; Festival 130; Prestige PR24029
5847	JAM–A–DITTY (Ellington)	Em 5327; Festival 130; Prestige PR24029

1947

Shelton Hemphill, Francis Williams, Harold Baker, Ray Nance, Dud Bascomb (tp); Lawrence Brown, Claude Jones, Tyree Glenn (tb); Russell Procope, Johnny Hodges, Jimmy Hamilton, Al Sears, Harry Carney (reeds); Fred Guy (g); Oscar Pettiford (b); Sonny Greer (d); Duke Ellington or Billy Strayhorn (p); Kay Davis, Al Hibbler, Dolores Parker (voc).* *Recorded Hollywood, August 14, 1947*

HC02531	HY'A SUE (Ellington)	CBS 88077, 66607
HC02532	LADY OF THE LAVENDER MIST (Ellington)	CBS 88077, 66607
HC02533	WOMEN (THEY'LL GET YOU) (Ellington; Latouche)* (RN)	CBS 88077, 66607

As above.		*Hollywood, September 1, 1947*
HC02596	IT'S MONDAY EVERY DAY (Robin) *(AH)	CBS 66607
HC02597	GOLDEN CRESS (Ellington; Brown)	CBS 88077, 66607
HC02598	PUT YOURSELF IN MY PLACE, BABY (Carmichael; Lane)	CBS 66607

As above, with Woody Herman (voc).		*Hollywood, September 29, 1947*
HC02654	COWBOY RHUMBA (Ellington; George; Relf) *(AH)	CBS 66607
HC02655	THE WILDEST GAL IN TOWN (Fain; Yellen)	CBS 66607
HC02656	I FELL AND BROKE MY HEART (Ellington; George)	CBS 66607

As above.		*Hollywood, September 30, 1947*
HC02658	YOU'RE JUST AN OLD ANTIDIS- ESTABLISHMENTARIANISMIST (Ellington; George)	CBS 66607
HC02662	DON'T BE SO MEAN BABY (Barbour; Lee)	CBS 66607

As above.   *Hollywood, October 1, 1947*
HC02663   IT'S MAD, MAD, MAD (Shaw; Higginbotham)   CBS 66607, 88077
HC02664   YOU GOTTA CRAWL BEFORE YOU   CBS 66607, 88077
          WALK (Ellington; Wells; Fotin; Tormé)

As above.   *Hollywood, October 2, 1947*
HC02666   KITTY (Weinstein; Brier)   CBS 66607, 88077
HC02667   BROWN PENNY (Ellington; Latouche)   CBS 66607, 88077

As above without Harold Baker.   *Hollywood, October 6, 1947*
HC02675   MAYBE I SHOULD CHANGE MY WAYS   CBS 66607, 88077
          (Ellington; Latouche)
HC02676   BOOGIE BOP BLUES (Ellington)   CBS 62993, 66607, 88077
HC02677   SULTRY SERENADE (Ellington)   CBS 88077, 66607

As above with Harold Baker (tp) & Wilbur de Paris (tb) added.
                                                        New York, November 10, 1947
CO38371   STOMP, LOOK AND LISTEN (Ellington)   CBS 66607, 88077
CO38372   AIR CONDITIONED JUNGLE   CBS 66607, 88077
          (Ellington; Hamilton)
CO38373   THREE CENT STOMP (Ellington)   CBS 66607, 88077

As above.   *New York, November 11, 1947.*
CO38374   PROGRESSIVE GAVOTTE (Strayhorn)   CBS 88077, 62993, 66607
CO38375   HE MAKES ME BELIEVE HE'S MINE   CBS 66607
          (Ellington; Latouche)

As above, without Wilbur de Paris (tb).   *New York, November 14, 1947*
CO38386   TAKE LOVE EASY (Ellington; Latouche)   CBS 66607, 88077
CO38387   I CAN'T BELIEVE THAT YOU'RE IN   CBS 66607, 62993, 88077
          LOVE WITH ME (McHugh; Gaskill)
CO38388   HOW HIGH THE MOON (Lewis; Hamilton)   CBS 66607,88077
CO38389   SINGIN' IN THE RAIN (Freed; Brown)   CBS 6607

As above but Herman Grimes (tp) replaces Baker & Edgar Brown (b) replaces
Pettiford.   *New York, November 18, 1947.*
CO38705   DO NOTHIN' TILL YOU HEAR FROM   CBS 66607, 64692, 52550;
          ME (Ellington; Russell)   A. Col. CS9629

As above but with Harold Baker (tp) & Oscar Pettiford (b) in place of Grimes &
Brown.   *New York, November 20, 1947.*
CO38398   DON'T GET AROUND MUCH ANYMORE   CBS 66607, 88077, 64692,
          (Ellington; Russell)   52550; A.Col. CS9629
CO38399   ONCE UPON A DREAM (Ellington;   CBS 66607
          Strayhorn; Hee; Cottrell)
CO38400   IT'S LOVE I'M IN (Ellington; Hee; Cottrell)   CBS 66607

As above, but Al Killian (tp) replaces Bascomb & Junior Raglin (b) added.
                                                        New York, December 22, 1947.
CO38591   I COULD GET A MAN (Ellington; Hee;   CBS 66607, 88077
          Cottrell)

Ray Nance (v); Lawrence Brown, Tyree Glenn (tb); Jimmy Hamilton, Johnny Hodges, Al Sears, Harry Carney (reeds); Junior Raglin (b); Sonny Greer (d); Duke Ellington (p); Dolores Parker (voc).   *New York, December 22, 1947.*
CO38592 ON A TURQUOISE CLOUD (Ellington;   CBS 88077, 66607
          Brown)

Shelton Hemphill, Francis Williams, Harold Baker, Al Killian, Ray Nance (tp); Lawrence Brown, Claude Jones, Tyree Glenn (tb); Jimmy Hamilton, Johnny Hodges, Russell Procope, Al Sears, Harry Carney (reeds); Duke Ellington (p); Fred Guy (g); Oscar Pettiford, Junior Raglin (b); Sonny Greer (d); Al Hibbler (voc).
                                              New York, December 24, 1947.
XCO   LIBERIAN SUITE:- I LIKE THE SUNRISE   CBS 62686, 66607
40789-94 & DANCES 1-5 (Ellington)

Harold Baker, Al Killian (t); Lawrence Brown (tb); Jimmy Hamilton, Johnny Hodges, Al Sears, Harry Carney (reeds); Junior Raglin (b); Duke Ellington, Billy Strayhorn (p); Sonny Greer (d); Dolores Parker (voc). *New York, December 30, 1947.*
CO38670 A WOMAN AND A MAN (Ellington; Russell)   CBS 66607

Harold Baker (tp); Johnny Hodges (a-s); Harry Carney (b-s); Duke Ellington (p); Junior Raglin (b); Sonny Greer (d).   *New York, December 30, 1947*
CO38671 THE CLOTHED WOMAN (Ellington)   CBS 88128, 66607

Al Killian, Harold Baker (tp); Lawrence Brown (tb); Jimmy Hamilton, Johnny Hodges, Al Sears, Harry Carney (reeds); Duke Ellington (p); Junior Raglin (bass); Sonny Greer (d).   *New York, December 30, 1947.*
CO38672 NEW YORK CITY BLUES (Ellington)   CBS 88128, 66607

Harold Baker, Al Killian (tp); Lawrence Brown, Tyree Glenn (tb); Johnny Hodges, Jimmy Hamilton, Al Sears (reeds); Duke Ellington (pno); Junior Raglin (b); Sonny Greer (d).   *New York, December 30, 1947.*
CO119017 LET'S GO BLUES (Ellington)   CBS 88128, 66607

The 1948 recording gap used to be filled by two LPs 'Ellington in Concert' Vols. 1 & 2 which were recorded at Cornell University in December 1948. Available as WRC T160 & T195.

1949
Harold Baker, Al Killian, Nelson Williams, Dave Burns, Ray Nance (tp); Lawrence Brown, Quentin Jackson, Tyree Glenn (tb); Johnny Hodges, Russell Procope, Jimmy Hamilton, Charlie Rouse, Jimmy Forrest, Harry Carney (reeds); Duke Ellington (p); Wendell Marshall (b); Sonny Greer (d); Kay Davis, Lu Elliot, Al Hibbler (voc).   *New York, September 1, 1949.*
CO41687 YOU OF ALL PEOPLE (Ellington)   CBS 66607
CO41688 CREOLE LOVE CALL (Ellington)   CBS 66607, 88128
CO41689 THE GREATEST THERE IS (Ellington)   CBS 66607, 88128
CO41690 SNIBOR (Strayhorn)   CBS 88128, 62993, 66607

Ray Nance (tp); Tyree Glenn (tb) (vib); Jimmy Hamilton, Johnny Hodges, Harry Carney (reeds); Wendell Marshall (b); Duke Ellington (p); Sonny Greer (d); Lu Elliot, Al Hibbler (voc). *New York, December 22, 1949.*

CO42550	THE WORLD IS WAITING FOR THE SUNRISE (Lockart; Scitz)	CBS 66607
CO42551	JOOG, JOOG (Ellington)	CBS 66607, 88128
CO42552	GOOD WOMAN BLUES (Ellington)	CBS 66607, 88128
CO42553	ON THE SUNNY SIDE OF THE STREET (McHugh; Fields)	CBS 66607, 88128
CO42554	B-SHARP BOSTON (Ellington)	CBS 88128, 62993, 66607

1950

Harold Baker, Nelson Williams, Fats Ford, Ray Nance, Cat Anderson (tp); Lawrence Brown, Quentin Jackson (tb); Mercer Ellington (Fr-h); Johnny Hodges, Russell Procope, Jimmy Hamilton, Paul Gonsalves, Harry Carney (reeds); Duke Ellington (p); Wendell Marshall (b); Sonny Greer (d); Al Hibbler, Yvonne Lanauze (voc). *New York, November 20, 1950.*

CO44662	BUILD THAT RAILROAD (Ellington)	CBS 66607, 88128
CO44663	LOVE YOU MADLY (Ellington)	CBS 66607, 88128
CO44664	GREAT TIMES (Ellington)	CBS 66607, 88128

As above with Tyree Glenn (tb) & Billy Strayhorn (p). *New York, December 18, 1950.*

5672	MOOD INDIGO (Ellington; Bigard; Mills)	CBS 63838, 84415
5672	SOPHISTICATED LADY (Ellington; Mills; DeLange)	CBS 63838, 84415

As above. *New York, December 19, 1950*

5673	THE TATTOOED BRIDE (Ellington)	CBS 63838, 84415
5673	SOLITUDE (Ellington; Mills; DeLange)	CBS 63838, 84415
	(4 titles issued on LP as 'MASTERPIECES BY ELLINGTON')	

1951

Harold Baker, Fats Ford, Cat Anderson, Nelson Williams, Ray Nance (tp); Juan Tizol, Britt Woodman, Quentin Jackson (tb); Willie Smith, Russell Procope, Jimmy Hamilton, Paul Gonsalves, Harry Carney (reeds); Duke Ellington (p); Wendell Marshall (b); Louis Bellson (d). *New York, May 10, 1951.*

CO45814	FANCY DAN (Ellington)	CBS 88128, 66607
CO45815	THE HAWK TALKS (Bellson)	CBS 88128, 66607
CO45816	V.I.P.'S BOOGIE (Ellington)	CBS 88128, 66607
CO45817	JAM WITH SAM (Ellington)	CBS 88128, 66607

Jimmy Hamilton, Willie Smith, Russell Procope, Harry Carney (clt); Wendell Marshall (b); Louis Bellson (d); Duke Ellington (narrator). *May 10, 1951*

CO45818	MONOLOGUE (PRETTY AND THE WOLF) (Hamilton; Ellington)	CBS 88128, 66607

Full band as above. *New York, May 24, 1951*

CO45829	TING-A-LING (Bellson; Shavers)	CBS 66607, 88128
CO45830	EIGHTH VEIL (Ellington; Strayhorn)	CBS 66607, 88128
CO45831	BROWN BETTY (Ellington; Strayhorn)	CBS 66607, 88128

113

As above without Ford & Anderson.   *New York, August 8, 1951.*
CO47018 DEEP NIGHT (Vallee; Henderson)   CBS 66607
CO47019 PLEASE BE KIND (Chaplin; Cahn)   CBS 66607
CO47020 SMADA (Ellington; Strayhorn)   CBS 66607
CO47021 ROCK SKIPPIN' AT THE BLUE NOTE   CBS 66607
          (Ellington; Strayhorn)

Harold Baker, Willie Cook, Francis Williams, Clark Terry, Dick Vance (tp); Britt
Woodman, Quentin Jackson, Juan Tizol (tb); Willie Smith, Russell Procope, Paul
Gonsalves, Jimmy Hamilton, Harry Carney (reeds); Wendell Marshall (b); Louis
Bellson (d); Duke Ellington or Billy Strayhorn (p); Lloyd Oldham (voc).
                                                            New York, December 7 1951.
CO47263 BENSONALITY (Ellington)   CBS 66607
LP*   A TONE PARALLEL TO HARLEM (THE   CCL830, 9, CBS 62686, 84309;
          HARLEM SUITE) (Ellington)   Ph BBL7003, 7443; A. Col. ML 463

As above, without Dick Vance.   *New York, December 11, 1951.*
CO47267 BLUES AT SUNDOWN (Ellington)   CBS 66607
CO47268 DUET (Ellington)   CBS 66607
CO47269 CONTROVERSIAL SUITE (Ellington)   CBS 66607
CO47270 AZALEA (Ellington)   CBS 66607
CO47271 VAGABONDS (Ellington; Tizol; Burke)   CBS 66607
CO47272 SOMETHING TO LIVE FOR (Ellington; Strayhorn)   CBS 66607

                                    1952
Cat Anderson, Clark Terry, Willie Cook, Ray Nance (tp); Quentin Jackson, Britt
Woodman, Juan Tizol (tb); Jimmy Hamilton, Russell Procope, Willie Smith, Paul
Gonsalves, Harry Carney (reeds); Duke Ellington (p); Wendell Marshall (b); Louis
Bellson (d).   *Seattle, Washington, March 25, 1952.*
SEATTLE CONCERT (LP)   RCA LJM-1002, F.RCA PM
          SKIN DEEP (Bellson); SULTRY   42852
          SERENADE (Ellington; Glenn);
          SOPHISTICATED LADY (Ellington;
          Mills; Parish); PERDIDO (Tizol);
          CARAVAN (Ellington; Tizol; Mills);
          HARLEM SUITE (Ellington); THE
          HAWK TALKS (Bellson); ELLINGTON
          MEDLEY (Ellington); JAM WITH SAM
          (Ellington)

Clark Terry, Cat Anderson (tp); Russell Procope, Paul Gonsalves, Harry Carney
(reeds); Duke Ellington (p); Wendell Marshall (b); Louis Bellson (d); Betty Roche
(voc).   *New York, June 30, 1952.*
CO47482 I LOVE MY LOVIN' LOVER (Ellington)   CBS 66607

Full band as above, except Hilton Jefferson replaces Smith, Betty Roche (voc).
                                                            New York, June 30, 1952.
CO47483 COME ON HOME (Ellington)   CBS 66607
LP*   TAKE THE 'A' TRAIN (Strayhorn)   Ph BBL7003, CBS 84309, 7443;
                                                          A. Col. ML-4639, CCL-830

As above.   *New York, July 1, 1952.*
LP*   PERDIDO (Tizol)   Ph BBL7003, 7443; CBS 84309;
                                                  A. Col. ML-4639, CCL-830
LP*   THE MOOCHE (Ellington; Mills)   Ph BBL7003, CBS 84309

As above.   *New York, August 10, 1952.*
LP*   SKIN DEEP (Bellson)   Ph BBL7003, 7443, CBS 84309;
                                                  A. Col. CCL830, ML4639
                    *the above items on LP 'ELLINGTON UP TOWN'

As above.   *New York, December, 1952*
CO48640   THE BLUES (Ellington)   CBS 66607
CO48641   BODY AND SOUL (Green; Eyton;   CBS 66607
          Sour; Heyman)

Willie Cook, Clark Terry, Ray Nance, John Carroll, John Hunt (tp); Britt
Woodman, Quentin Jackson, Fred Johnson (tb); Russell Procope, Porter Kilbert,
Jimmy Hamilton, Paul Gonsalves, Harry Carney (reeds); Duke Ellington (p);
Wendell Marshall (b); Louis Bellson (d); Jimmy Grissom (voc).
                                            Chicago, December 22, 1952.
CC05397   PRIMPIN' FOR THE PROM (Ellington)   CBS 62993, 66607
CC05398   THE VULTURE SONG (Chase)   CBS 66607
CC05399   FOLLOW ME (Ellington)   CBS 66607

                                  1953
Duke Ellington (p); Wendell Marshall (b); Butch Ballard (d).
                                          Hollywood, April 13/14, 1953.
DUKE MEETS ELLINGTON: WHO KNOWS   Capitol LC6670 *WRC T708
          (Ellington); B SHARP BLUES
          (Ellington); *PASSION FLOWER
          (Strayhorn; Ellington);
          REFLECTIONS IN D (Ellington);
          *PRELUDE TO A KISS (Ellington;
          Mills; Kurtz); THINGS AIN'T WHAT
          THEY USED TO BE (M. Ellington;
          Persons); JANET (Ellington)

Ray Nance, Cat Anderson, Clark Terry, Willie Cook (tp); Juan Tizol, Quentin
Jackson, Britt Woodman (tb); Harry Carney, Jimmy Hamilton, Russell Procope,
Paul Gonsalves, Rick Henderson (reeds); Duke Ellington (p); Wendell Marshall,
(b); Butch Ballard (d).   *New York, December 21, 1953.*
          FLYING HOME (Goodman; Hampton;   *Cap LCT6008; A. Cap W521,
          Robin)   TS21
          HONEYSUCKLE ROSE (Waller; Razaf)   *Cap LCT6008; A. Cap W521,
                                                                     TS21

                                                                      115

As above.   *Chicago, December 28, 1953.*
    NIGHT TIME (Ellington; Strayhorn)
    STOMPIN' AT THE SAVOY (Sampson;   *Cap LCT6008; A. Cap W521,
    Goodman; Webb; Razaf)   TS21
As above.   *Chicago, December 29, 1953.*
    DON'T EVER SAY GOODBYE (Ellington)   ; Cap T679, WRC T309
    BLACK AND TAN FANTASY (Miley;   *Cap LCT6008; A. Cap W521,
    Ellington)   TS21; WRCT708

1954

As above.   *Chicago, January 1, 1954.*
    IN THE MOOD (Garland; Razaf)   *Cap LCT6008; A. Cap W521, TS21

As above.   *Chicago, January 2, 1954.*
    ONE O'CLOCK JUMP (Basie)   *Cap LCT6008; A. Cap W521, TS21

As above.   *Chicago, January 17, 1954.*
    HAPPY-GO-LUCKY LOCAL   *Cap LCT6008; A. Cap W521,
    (Ellington)   TS21
    ROCKIN' IN RHYTHM (Carney;   *Cap LCT6008, WRC T708;
    Ellington; Mills)   A. Cap W521, TS21
    FALLING LIKE A RAINDROP (Ellington)   Cap T679, WRC T309

  *The items above on LCT6008 issued collectively as **ELLINGTON '55**. LP re-issued on
Capitol SC 062 80.270.

Ray Nance, Clark Terry, Willie Cook, Cat Anderson, Gerald Wilson (tp); Quentin
Jackson, Britt Woodman, John Sanders (tb); Jimmy Hamilton, Rick Henderson,
Russell Procope, Paul Gonsalves, Harry Carney (reeds); Duke Ellington (p); Billy
Strayhorn (p); Wendell Marshall (b); Dave Black (d); Robert Collier (conga).

                                              San Francisco, April 26, 1954.
    ALL DAY LONG (Strayhorn)   Cap WRC TP86
    BUNNY HOP MAMBO (Anthony; Auletti)   Cap WRC TP86
    ISLE OF CAPRI (Kennedy; Grosz)   Cap WRC TP86
    BAND CALL (Ellington)   Cap WRC TP86

Same, without Collier & Wilson.   *New York, June 17, 1954.*
    GONNA TAN YOUR HIDE (Ellington;   CapT670, WRC T309
    Strayhorn)

Same as above.   *Hollywood, September 1, 1954.*
    SMILE (Chaplin)   Cap WRC TP86
    TYROLEAN TANGO (Stewart)   Cap WRC TP86
    IF I GIVE MY HEART TO YOU (Brewster)   Cap WRC TP86
    CHILE BOWL (Ellington)   Cap WRC TP86
    BAKIFF (Ellington; Tizol)   Cap WRC T708

Same as above, except Oscar Pettiford replaces Marshall. *Chicago, October 8, 1954.*
    TWELFTH STREET RAG-MAMBO (Bowman)   Cap WRC TP86
    CARAVAN (Ellington; Tizol)   Cap WRC T708

1955

As above, except that Jimmy Woods replaces Pettiford. *Chicago, May 17/18, 1955.*
    LA VIRGEN DE LA MACARENA   Cap T679 WRC T309
    (Monterde; Calero)
    HARLEM AIR-SHAFT (Ellington)   Cap T679 WRC T309
    CLARINET MELODRAMA (Hamilton)   Cap T679 WRC T309
    THEME FOR TRAMBEAM (Hamilton)   Cap T679 WRC T309
    SERIOUS SERENADE (Ellington)   Cap T679 WRC T309

1956

Willie Cook, Clark Terry, Cat Anderson, Ray Nance (tp & vln); Quentin Jackson, John Sanders, Britt Woodman (tb); Johnny Hodges, Paul Gonsalves, Russell Procope, Jimmy Hamilton, Harry Carney (reeds); Duke Ellington (p); Jimmy Woode (b); Sam Woodward (d); Ray Nance & Jimmy Grissom (voc).

Chicago, February 7/8, 1956.

HISTORICALLY SPEAKING - THE DUKE: Lon LTZ-N15029; A. Beth
    EAST ST. LOUIS TOODLE-OO   BCP-6003;
    (Ellington; Miley); CREOLE LOVE   as STOMP LOOK AND LISTEN -
    CALL (Ellington; Miley; Jackson);   Emb CJS-809; as THE BIG BAND
    STOMPY JONES (Ellington); THE JEEP   SOUND OF DUKE ELLINGTON -
    IS JUMPIN' (Ellington; Hodges);   Pol 2941 202; as THE
    JACK THE BEAR (Ellington); IN A   BETHLEHEM YEARS, Vol 1 - CBS
    MELLOW TONE (Ellington; Gabler);   82108; A. Beth BCP-60,
    KO-KO (Ellington); MIDRIFF   BTM6804
    (Strayhorn); STOMP, LOOK AND   as THE JEEP IS JUMPIN
    LISTEN (Ellington); UNBOOTED   A. Affinity AFF91
    CHARACTER (Ellington); LONESOME
    LULLABY (Ellington); UPPER
    MANHATTAN MEDICAL GROUP
    (Ellington)

As above.   *Same dates.*
DUKE ELLINGTON PRESENTS: Lon LTZ-N15078; Par
    SUMMERTIME (Gershwin; Heyward)   PMC1136; A. Beth BPC-6005;
    LAURA (Mercer; Raksin); I CAN'T   as COTTONTAIL - Ember CJS-
    GET STARTED (Duke; Gershwin);   813; Polydor 54515;
    MY FUNNY VALENTINE (Rodgers;   Affinity AFS 1013; as
    Hart); EVERYTHING BUT YOU   THE BETHLEHEM YEARS, Vol 2-
    (Ellington; James; George);   Beth BTH6805
    FRUSTRATION (Ellington); COTTON
    TAIL (Ellington); DAY DREAM
    (Strayhorn; Ellington; LaTouche);
    DEEP PURPLE (DeRose; Parish);
    INDIAN SUMMER (Herbert; Dubin);
    BLUES (Ellington).

117

As above, with Lawrence Brown (tb) added & Billy Strayhorn replacing Ellington.

New York, March 1956.

ELLINGTONIA '56: THE HAPPY ONE   Columbia 33CX10055; A. Verve
(Anderson); DUKE'S JAM (Hodges);
NIGHT WALK (Anderson); YOU GOT
IT COMING (Hodges).

Ray Nance (tp); Lawrence Brown (tb); Jimmy Hamilton, Johnny Hodges, Harry
Carney (reeds); Billy Strayhorn (p); Jimmy Woode (b); Sam Woodyard (d).

Same date.

HI'YA (Hodges); SNIBOR
(Strayhorn); TEXAS BLUES (Hodges).   Columbia 33CX10055; A. Verve

Full band as above.   *Newport, July 7, 1956.*
ELLINGTON AT NEWPORT: NEWPORT JAZZ   Ph BBL7133/SBBL526; A. Col.
FESTIVAL SUITE (Ellington;   CL-934/CS-8648; CBS 65113,
Hodges); DIMINUENDO AND   84403, F.CBS 63531
CRESCENDO IN BLUE (Ellington)

As above.   *Newport, July 7, 1956.*
DUKE ELLINGTON AT NEWPORT: TAKE   Ph BBL7152; A. Col CL-933;
THE 'A' TRAIN (Strayhorn);   CBS 84420
SOPHISTICATED LADY (Ellington;
Mills; Parish); I GOT IT BAD AND
THAT AIN'T GOOD (Ellington;
Webster); SKIN DEEP (Bellson).

Clark Terry, Ray Nance (tp); Quentin Jackson (tb); Jimmy Hamilton, Johnny
Hodges, Harry Carney (reeds); Billy Strayhorn (p); Jimmy Woode (b); Sam
Woodyard (d).   *New York, October, 1956.*
JOHNNY HODGES AND THE   Columbia 33CX10098;
ELLINGTON ALL-STARS: MEET MR.   A. Verve
RABBIT (Hodges); DUKE'S IN BED
(Ellington); JUST SQUEEZE ME
(Ellington); CONFAB WITH RAB
(Hodges); AH ODDIE OOBIE
(Hodges); BALLADE FOR VERY SAD
AND VERY TIRED LOTUS EATERS
(Strayhorn); IT HAD TO BE YOU
(Jones; Cahn); BLACK AND TAN
FANTASY (Miley; Ellington); TAKE
THE 'A' TRAIN (Strayhorn).

Cat Anderson, Clark Terry, Ray Nance, Willie Cook (tp); Britt Woodman, Quentin
Jackson, John Sanders (tb); Jimmy Hamilton, Johnny Hodges, Russell Procope,
Paul Gonsalves, Rick Henderson, Harry Carney (reeds); Duke Ellington (p); Jimmy
Woode (b); Sam Woodyard (d); Candido, Terry Snyder (per); Betty Glamman
(harp); Joya Sherrill, Margaret Tynes, Ozzie Bailey (voc); Chorus; Ellington
(narrator).   *New York, September 17/24/25/28, October 22/23, December 6, 1956.*
A DRUM IS A WOMAN (Ellington; Strayhorn)   Ph BBL7179; A. Col JCL-951;
CBS 65185, 84404

Full band as above, Rick Henderson (alto) added on * and Harold Baker (tp) added on * and **.

New York, March 13, *September 9, ** October 1, 10, 14, 1957.

SOLITUDE: *THE SKY FELL DOWN (Ellington); *MOOD INDIGO (Ellington; Bigard); *TENDERLY; (Gross); **AUTUMN LEAVES (Kosma); **PRELUDE TO A KISS (Ellington); **DANCING IN THE DARK (Schwartz); **WHERE AND WHEN (Rodgers); **WILLOW WEEP FOR ME (Ronnell); **SOLITUDE (Ellington)

Ph BBL7229/SBBL532;
A. Col CL-1085 CBS 63363;
as INDIGOS-CBS C58053

As above. *New York, August 7, 1956, April 15, May 3, 1957.*

SUCH SWEET THUNDER (Ellington; Strayhorn)

PhBBL7203
A. Col JCL-1033/CS-8091;
CBS 52421; 84405

As above, except that Harold Baker replaces Willie Cook, Bill Graham replaces Hodges. Mahalia Jackson (voc). *New York, Feb 5, 11, 12, 1958.*

BLACK, BROWN AND BEIGE (Ellington)

Phi BBL7251/SBBL506;
A. Col CL-1162/JCS-8015; CBS 63363; 84406

Cat Anderson, Clark Terry, Harold Baker, John Cook (tp); Ray Nance (tp/vln); Britt Woodman, Quentin Jackson, John Sanders (tb); Johnny Hodges, Russell Procope, Bill Graham, Paul Gonsalves, Jimmy Hamilton, Harry Carney (reeds); Duke Ellington (p); Jimmy Woode (b); Sam Woodyard (d).

New York, March 24, 26, 31 & April 1, 1958.

BAL MASQUE: ALICE BLUE GOWN (Tierney; McCarthy); WHO'S AFRAID OF THE BIG BAD WOLF (Churchill; Ronell); GOT A DATE WITH AN ANGEL (Waller; Tunbridge; Grey; Miller); POOR BUTTERFLY (Hubbell; Golden); SPOOKY TAKES A HOLIDAY (Ellington); THE PEANUT VENDOR (Simons; Gilbert; Sunshine); SATIN DOLL (Ellington); LADY IN BED (Wrubel; Dixon); INDIAN LOVE CALL (Friml; Harbach; Hammerstein); DONKEY SERENADE (Friml; Stothart; Wright; Forrest); GYPSY LOVE SONG (Herbert; Smith); LAUGH, CLOWN, LAUGH (Lewis; Young; Fiorito).

Philips BBL7315/SBBL543;
CBS 63513; A. Col CL1282/
CS8098; 84409

Cat Anderson, Harold Baker, Andre Merenguito Forda, Willie Cook, Clark Terry (tp); Ray Nance (tp/vln); Britt Woodman, Quentin Jackson (tb); Paul Gonsalves, Jimmy Hamilton, Johnny Hodges, Russell Procope, Harry Carney (reeds); Duke Ellington (p); Jimmy Woode, Joe Benjamin (b); Sam Woodyard, Jimmy Johnson (d).   *New York, September 8, 1958.*

FESTIVAL SESSION: DUAEL FUEL Pts. 1-3   Ph. BBL7355/SBBL556;
(Ellington; Terry); IDIOM '59, Pts. 1-3   A. Col CL-1400/CS-8200;
(Ellington); LAUNCHING PAD   CBS 64063; 21137
(Ellington; Terry); COP-OUT
EXTENSION (Ellington); THINGS
AIN'T WHAT THEY USED TO BE
(M. Ellington); PERDIDO (Ellington; Tizol).

1959

                                                As above. New York, 1959, 71, 72.
THE QUEEN'S SUITE (Ellington) (1959)/   Pol 2335 743; A. Pablo 2310 762;
GOUTELAS SUITE (Ellington) (1971)/   as THE ELLINGTON SUITES
UWIS SUITE (Ellington) (1972)

Cat Anderson, Clark Terry, Harold Baker, John Cook (tp); Ray Nance (tp/vln); Britt Woodman, Quentin Jackson, John Sanders (tb); Johnny Hodges, Russell Procope, Bill Graham, Paul Gonsalves, Jimmy Hamilton, Harry Carney (reeds); Duke Ellington (p); Jimmy Woode (b); Sam Woodyard (d).
                                                Recorded New York, December 2, 1959.
BLUES IN ORBIT: THREE J'S BLUES; SMADA;   Ph.BBL7381/SBBL567; A. Col
PIE EYE'S BLUES; SWEET AND   CL-1445; CBS 84307
PUNGENT; C JAM BLUES; IN A MELLOW
TONE; BLUES IN BLUEPRINT; THE
SWINGERS GET THE BLUES TOO; THE
SWINGER'S JUMP; BLUES IN ORBIT;
VILLES VILLE IS THE BEST PLACE, MAN.

1962

Ray Nance (c & vln); Lawrence Brown (tb); Johnny Hodges (alt); Coleman Hawkins (ten); Harry Carney (bar); Duke Ellington (p); Aaron Bell (b); Sam Woodyard (d).   *New York, August 18, 1962.*
THE DUKE MEETS COLEMAN HAWKINS: A. Impulse S-26; AS-26;
LIMBO JAZZ (Ellington); MOOD   WRC T/ST489
INDIGO (Ellington; Mills; Bigard);
RAY CHARLES' PLACE (Ellington);
WANDERLUST (Ellington; Hodges);
YOU DIRTY DOG (Ellington); SELF
PORTRAIT (OF THE BEAN) (Ellington;
Strayhorn); THE JEEP IS JUMPIN'
(Ellington; Hodges); THE RICITIC
(Ellington).

Cootie Williams, Cat Anderson, Roy Burrows, Ray Nance (tp); Lawrence Brown,
Buster Cooper, Chuck Connors (tb); Johnny Hodges, Russell Procope, Jimmy
Hamilton, Paul Gonsalves, Harry Carney (reeds); Duke Ellington (p); Ernie
Shepard (b); Sam Woodyard (d).

Chicago, November 29, New York, December 13, 14, 20, 29, 1962 & January 4, 1963.

RECOLLECTIONS OF THE BIG BAND ERA: Atlantic SD 1665,
        MINNIE THE MOOCHER; FOR   ATL50 110
        DANCERS ONLY; IT'S A LONESOME
        OLD TOWN; CHEROKEE; THE
        MIDNIGHT SUN WILL NEVER SET;
        LET'S GET TOGETHER; I'M GETTING
        SENTIMENTAL OVER YOU; CHANT OF
        THE WEED; CIRIBIRIBIN; CONTRASTS;
        CHRISTOPHER COLUMBUS; AULD
        LANG SYNE.

1963

Cootie Williams, Cat Anderson, Roy Burrows (tp); Ray Nance (c, vln); Lawrence
Brown, Buster Cooper, Chuck Connors (tb); Johnny Hodges, Russell Procope,
Jimmy Hamilton, Paul Gonsalves, Harry Carney (reeds); Duke Ellington (p); Ernie
Shepard (b); Sam Woodyard (d).   *Paris, January 2, 1963.*

THE ART OF DUKE ELLINGTON: KINDA   Atlantic ATL 60 044 (2);
        DUKISH (Ellington); ROCKIN' IN   AS THE GREAT PARIS CONCERT
        RHYTHM (Carney; Ellington; Mills);   At SD 2-304 (2)
        ON THE SUNNY SIDE OF THE STREET
        (McHugh; Fields); THE STAR-
        CROSSED LOVERS (Ellington); ALL OF
        ME (Simons, Marks); THEME FROM
        'ASPHALT JUNGLE' (Ellington);
        CONCERTO FOR COOTIE (Ellington;
        Russell); TUTTI FOR COOTIE
        (Ellington); SUITE THURSDAY
        (Ellington); PERDIDO (Tizol); THE
        EIGHTH VEIL (Ellington); ROSE OF
        THE RIO GRANDE (Leslie; Warren;
        Gorman); COP OUT (Ellington);
        BULA/JAM WITH SAM (Ellington);
        HAPPY-GO-LUCKY LOCAL (Ellington)
        TONE PARALLEL TO HARLEM
        (Ellington).

1965

Duke Ellington, Billy Taylor, Charles Bell, Earl Hines, Mary Lou Williams, Willie
'The Lion' Smith (p).   *Pittsburgh, June 20, 1965.*

THE JAZZ PIANO: THE SECOND PORTRAIT OF   RCA SF-7830;
        THE LION (Ellington); HOUSE OF   A.RCA LSP-3499
        LORDS (Ellington & Hines); SWEET
        LORRAINE (Ellington; Hines &
        Taylor); etc.

Cootie Williams, Cat Anderson, Mercer Ellington, Herbie Jones (tp); Lawrence Brown, Buster Cooper, Quentin Jackson, Charles Connors (tb); Harry Carney, Russell Procope, Johnny Hodges, Jimmy Hamilton, Paul Gonsalves (reeds); Duke Ellington (p); John Lamb (b); Louis Bellson (d); Brock Peters, Esther Marrow, Jimmy McPhial (voc); Bunny Briggs (dancer); The Herman McCoy Choir.

Recorded New York, December 26, 1965.

CONCERT OF SACRED MUSIC: (Ellington):   RCA RD/SF-7811;
    IN THE BEGINNING GOD; TELL ME IT'S   A.RCA LSP-3582;
    THE TRUTH; COME SUNDAY; THE   RCA PL43663
    LORD'S PRAYER; COME SUNDAY; WILL
    YOU BE THERE?; AIN'T BUT THE ONE;
    NEW WORLD A-COMING; DAVID
    DANCED BEFORE THE LORD WITH ALL
    HIS MIGHT.

1966

Duke Ellington (p); John Lamb (b); Sam Woodyard (d).   *New York, July 18, 1966.*
(see also 1970)

THE PIANIST: DON JUAN (Ellington); SLOW BLUES   Fantasy F9462;
    (Ellington); LOOKING GLASS   Metronome 0061 153
    (Ellington); THE SHEPHERD
    (Ellington); TAP DANCER'S BLUES;
    SAM WOODYARD'S BLUES (Ellington).

Cootie Williams, Cat Anderson, Mercer Ellington, Herbie Jones (tp); Lawrence Brown, Buster Cooper, Chuck Connors (tb); Harry Carney, Russell Procope, Johnny Hodges, Jimmy Hamilton, Paul Gonsalves (reeds); Duke Ellington (p); John Lamb (b); Rufus Jones (d).   *Recorded New York, December, 1966.*
FAR EAST SUITE: (Ellington &   RCA SF-7894; LSA-3063
    Strayhorn): TOURIST POINT OF   A.RCA LSP-3782/LSP-3782;
    VIEW; BLUEBIRD OF DELHI (MYNAH);   RCA PL45699; J.RCA RJL 2533
    ISFAHAN; DEPK; MOUNT HARISSA;
    BLUE PEPPER (FAR EAST OF THE
    BLUES); AGRA; AMAD; AD LIB ON
    NIPPON.

1967

Cootie Williams, Cat Anderson, Mercer Ellington, Herbie Jones (tp); Lawrence Brown, Buster Cooper, Chuck Connors (tb); Harry Carney, Russell Procope, Johnny Hodges, Jimmy Hamilton, Paul Gonsalves (reeds); Duke Ellington (p); John Lamb (b); Sam Woodyard (d).   *Hollywood, 1967.*
THE POPULAR DUKE ELLINGTON: TAKE   RCA SF-7835; LSA-3072;
    THE 'A' TRAIN (Strayhorn); I GOT IT   A.RCA LSP-3576; INTS5006;
    BAD AND THAT AIN'T GOOD   F.RCA FX L1-7104;
    (Ellington; Webster); PERDIDO   RCA CL43288
    (Tizol; Drake; Lenk); MOOD INDIGO
    (Ellington; Mills; Bigard); BLACK
    AND TAN FANTASY (Ellington;
    Miley); THE TWITCH (Ellington)

SOLITUDE (Ellington; De Lange;
Mills); DO NOTHIN' TILL YOU HEAR
FROM ME (Ellington; Russell); THE
MOOCHE (Ellington; Mills);
SOPHISTICATED LADY (Ellington;
Mills; Parish); CREOLE LOVE CALL
(Ellington).

Cat Anderson, Mercer Ellington, Herbie Jones, Cootie Williams (tp); Clark Terry
(fh); Lawrence Brown, Buster Cooper, Chuck Connors (tb); Johnny Hodges,
Russell Procope, Jimmy Hamilton, Paul Gonsalves, Harry Carney (reeds); Duke
Ellington (p); Aaron Bell (b); Steve Little (d).   *New York, August 28, 1967.*
AND HIS MOTHER CALLED HIM BILL:
    BOO-DAH (Strayhorn);   RCA SF-7964, LSA-3073; A.RCA LPM-3906/
    U.M.M.G. (Strayhorn)   LSP-3906; J.RCA RJL2534; *NL89166

As above, without Terry.
    BLOOD COUNT (Strayhorn); SMADA (Strayhorn)*

As above, with John Saunders (tb).   *August 30, 1967.*
    RAIN CHECK (Strayhorn); ROCK SKIPPIN' AT THE
    BLUE NOTE (Strayhorn; Ellington); MY LITTLE
    BROWN BOOK (Strayhorn)*

Duke Ellington (p).
    LOTUS BLOSSOM (Strayhorn)

As above.   *September 1, 1957.*
    SNIBOR (Strayhorn); AFTER ALL (Strayhorn);
    ALL DAY LONG (Strayhorn)

As above, except Jeff Castleman (b) & Sam Woodyard (d) replace Aaron Bell &
Steve Little.   *San Francisco, November 16, 1967.*
    CHARPOY (Strayhorn); THE INTIMACY OF THE BLUES
    (Strayhorn); DAY-DREAM (Strayhorn; Ellington)

1968
Cat Anderson, Herbie Jones, Cootie Williams, Mercer Ellington (tp); Lawrence
Brown, Buster Cooper, Chuck Connors (tb); Russell Procope, Johnny Hodges,
Jimmy Hamilton, Paul Gonsalves, Harry Carney (reeds); Duke Ellington (p); Jeff
Castleman (b); Sam Woodyard (d).   *New Haven, Conn., January 26 1968.*
YALE CONCERT: THE LITTLE PURPLE FLOWER   Fantasy F9433
    (Ellington); PUT-TIN (Ellington;
    Strayhorn); A CHROMATIC LOVE
    AFFAIR (Ellington); BOOLA, BOOLA
    (Ellington); DRAG (Ellington);
    SALOME (Ellington); SWAMP GOO
    (Ellington); UP-JUMP (Ellington);
    TAKE THE 'A' TRAIN (Strayhorn).

Cat Anderson, Willie Cook, Cootie Williams, Mercer Ellington (tp); Lawrence Brown, Buster Cooper, Chuck Connors (tb); Russell Procope; Johnny Hodges, Harold Ashby, Paul Gonsalves, Harry Carney (reeds); Duke Ellington (p); Jeff Castleman (b); Rufus Jones (d). *New York, November 5, 1968.*

LATIN-AMERICAN SUITE (Ellington): Fantasy F-8419
    OCLUPACA; CHICO CUADRADINO;
    EQUE; THE SLEEPING LADY AND THE
    GIANT WHO WATCHES OVER HER;
    LATIN AMERICAN SUNSHINE;
    BRASILLIANCE.

1970

Duke Ellington (p); Victor Gaskin, Paul Kondziela (b); Rufus Jones (d).
Las Vegas, January 7, 1970. (see also 1966)

THE PIANIST: DUCK AMOK (Ellington); NEVER Fantasy F9462;
    STOP REMEMBERING, BILL Metronome 0061 153
    (Ellington); FAT MESS (Ellington).

As above. *(see also 1968)*
    TINA (Ellington) Fantasy F8419

Cootie Williams, Harold Johnson, Mercer Ellington, Al Rubin, Fred Stone (t) (fl-h); 'Booty' Wood, Julian Priestwood, Dave Taylor (tb); Russell Procope, Norris Turney, Harold Ashby, Harry Carney, Johnny Hodges, Paul Gonsalves (reeds); Duke Ellington (p); Joe Benjamin (b); Rufus Jones (d). *New York, April 27, 1970.*

NEW ORLEANS SUITE (Ellington): BOURBON Atlantic 2400 135;
    STREET JINGLING JOLLIES; THANKS FOR A. Atlantic SD-1580,
    THE BEAUTIFUL LAND ON THE DELTA; SECOND K 40209, K50403
    LINE; ARISTOCRACY A LA JEAN LAFITTE;
    As above, with Wild Bill Davis (org)
    added: BLUES FOR NEW ORLEANS.
    As above, except Cat Anderson (t)
    replaces Johnson & Chuck Connors
    (tb) replaces Taylor & without
    Johnny Hodges: PORTRAIT OF LOUIS
    ARMSTRONG; PORTRAIT OF
    WELLMAN BRAUD; PORTRAIT OF
    SIDNEY BECHET;PORTRAIT OF
    MAHALIA JACKSON.

1971

Cootie Williams, John Coles, Mercer Ellington, Harold Johnson (tp); Chuck Connors, Malcolm Taylor, Mitchell 'Booty' Wood (tb); Harry Carney, Russell Procope, Norris Turney, Paul Gonsalves, Harold Ashby, Harold Minerve (reeds); Duke Ellington (p); Joe Benjamin (b); Rufus Jones (d); Nell Brookshire (voc).
Bristol, October 22 & Birmingham, October 24, 1971.

THE ENGLISH CONCERT: TOGO SUITE (TOGO U-A UAD60032/3;
    BRAVA) (Ellington); C-JAM BLUES A. Sunset SLD507/8
    (Ellington); HAPPY REUNION
    (Ellington); ADDI (Ellington);

LOTUS BLOSSOM (Strayhorn);
COTTON TAIL (Ellington);
CHECKERED HAT (Ellington);
LA PLUS BELLE AFRICAINE
(Ellington); IN A MELLOW TONE
(Ellington); I GOT IT BAD (Ellington;
Webster); GOOF (Ellington); SOUL
FLUTE (FLUTE AME) (Ellington).

1973
Duke Ellington (p); Joe Pass (g); Ray Brown (b); Louis Bellson (d).
New York, January 8, 1973.
DUKE'S BIG FOUR: COTTONTAIL (Ellington);   Pablo 2310 703
THE BLUES (Ellington); THE HAWK
TALKS (Bellson); PRELUDE TO A KISS
(Ellington); LOVE YOU MADLY
(Ellington); JUST SQUEEZE ME
(Ellington); EVERYTHING BUT YOU
(Ellington; James; George).

Mercer Ellington, Harold Johnson, Johnny Coles, Barry Lee Hall (tp); Vince
Prudente, Art Baron, Chuck Connors (tb); Harry Carney, Harold Minerve, Russell
Procope, Harold Ashby, Percy Marion (reeds); Duke Ellington (p); Joe Benjamin
(b); Quentin White (d); Alice Babs, Toney Watkins (voc); John Alldis Choir.
London, October 24, 1973.
THIRD SACRED CONCERT (Ellington):   RCA SF-8406; A.RCA, APL1-0785
INTRODUCTION; THE LORD'S
PRAYER; MY LOVE; IS GOD A THREE
LETTER WORD FOR LOVE; THE
BROTHERHOOD; HALLELUJAH;
EVERY MAN PRAYS IN HIS OWN
LANGUAGE; AIN'T NOBODY NOWHERE
NOTHIN' WITHOUT GOD; THE
MAJESTY OF GOD.

Mercer Ellington, Harold Johnson, Johnny Coles, Barry Lee Hall (tp); Vince
Prudente, Art Baron, Chuck Connors (tb); Harry Carney, Russell Procope, Harold
Minerve, Harold Ashby, Percy Marion (reeds); Duke Ellington (p); Joe Benjamin
(b); Rocky White (d); Anita Moore, Harold 'Money' Johnson (voc).
Eastbourne, December 1, 1973.
EASTBOURNE PERFORMANCE: THE PIANO   RCA SF-8447, 6310
PLAYER; CREOLE LOVE CALL; DON'T   A.RCA APLI-1023;
YOU KNOW I CARE; I CAN'T GET   J.RCA P634
STARTED; NEW YORK, NEW YORK;
PITTER PATTER PANTHER; HOW
HIGH THE MOON; BASIN STREET
BLUES; TIGER RAG; WOODS;
MEDITATION.

Other LPs currently available

THE DUKE ELLINGTON MEMORIAL ALBUM VOL. 1 – 1920-37 – BYG 6641 247
THIS IS DUKE ELLINGTON – 1927-45 – RCA 26 28036
REFLECTIONS IN ELLINGTON (Stereo) – 1932-50 – Everybody's 3005
DUKE ELLINGTON IN THE 40s (with Blanton) – 1940-41 – RCA NL47357
THE JIMMY BLANTON YEARS – October 1940-June 1941 – Queen Disc 007
THE UNCOLLECTED DUKE ELLINGTON Vols. 1-5 – 1946-47 Decca 6.23575-9
CARNEGIE HALL CONCERT 1948 Vols. 1&2 – November 13, 1948
  – Jazz Anthology 30 JA5140/1
PIANO REFLECTIONS – April/December 1953 – Capitol 5C 052.80851
DUKE ELLINGTON AT TANGLEWOOD Vols. 1&2 – July 15, 1956
  – Queen Disc 049/050
DUKE 56/62 (3 double-LPs of many unissued items & alternative takes)
  – CBS 88653, 88654, 26306
THE COSMIC SCENE – April 2/3, 1958 – CBS 84407
NEWPORT JAZZ FESTIVAL – July 3, 1958 – CBS 84408
JAZZ AT THE PLAZA – 1958 – CBS 32471
ELLINGTON JAZZ PARTY – February 19, 1959 – CBS 88410
ELLINGTON '59 – March 27, 1959 – Fairmont 107
UNKNOWN SESSION July 14, 1960 – CBS 82819
PIANO IN THE BACKGROUND/FOREGROUND – June 1960/March 1, 1961
  – CBS 84418/9 or 67252
FIRST TIME! THE COUNT MEETS THE DUKE – July 6, 1961 – CBS 84417
DUKE ELLINGTON & JOHN COLTRANE – September 26, 1962 – Impulse AS-30
THE IMPULSE YEARS – Vol. 1 (1962-64)/Vol. 2 (1966-73)
  – Impulse 92562 & 92852
MONEY JUNGLE (with Mingus & Roach) – September 17, 1962
  – Blue Note BNP25113
WILL BIG BANDS EVER COME BACK – November/December 1962 – Reprise 6168
ELLINGTON FOR ALWAYS (with Symphony Orchestra)
  – January/February 1963 – Stanyan 10105
THE DUKE AT TANGLEWOOD – July 28, 1963 – RCA PJL1-8075

MY PEOPLE – August/September 1963 – Philips 6369 400
or Flying Dutchman 10112
ELLINGTON '65 – April 1964 – Reprise 6122
CONCERT IN THE VIRGIN ISLANDS – April 14, 1965 – Reprise 6185
ELLA AT DUKE'S PLACE (Ella Fitzgerald) – October/November 1965
– Verve V6-4070
DUKE SOLO – February 25, 1966 – President KVP225
COLLAGES (with Ron Collier) – July 24/25, 1967 – MPS 68049
SECOND SACRED CONCERT – 1968 America AM006/007
THE INTIMATE ELLINGTON – April 1969/June 1971 – Pablo 2310 787
UP IN DUKE'S WORKSHOP – April 1969/December 1972 – Pablo 2310 815
THE AFRO-EURASIAN ECLIPSE – February 17, 1971 – Fantasy F-9498
THIS ONE'S FOR BLANTON – December 5, 1973 – Pablo 2310 721

Ellington on Compact Disc

DUKE ELLINGTON AT THE BLUE NOTE – Vogue VG600062
SIDE BY SIDE (with Hodges) – Verve 821 578-2
BACK TO BACK (with Hodges) – Starr 823 637-2
DUKE ELLINGTON IN THE SIXTIES – RCA PD89565
HARLEM – Pablo CD2308-245
SRO – Inner City C38-7680
ELLINGTON '56 – Charley CD20
DUKE'S BIG FOUR – Pablo J33J20009
THE ELLINGTON SUITES – Pablo J33J20008
THIS ONE'S FOR BLANTON – Pablo J33J20010